CW00404040

The Wilts & Berks Canal

by
L.J. Dalby

THE OAKWOOD PRESS

© Oakwood Press & Wilts & Berks Canal Amenity Group 2000

British Library Cataloguing in Publication Data
A Record for this book is available from the British Library
ISBN 0 85361 562 4

Printed by Oakdale Printing Co., Poole, Dorset.

First Edition published in 1971
Reprinted 1974
Second Edition 1986
Reprinted 1989
Third Edition 2000

A boat enters the Wilts & Berks Canal at Abingdon.

Front cover, top: Peaceful cruising at Templar's Firs.   *D.G. & B.A. Small*
Front cover, bottom: West Mill lift bridge near Cricklade *c.*1900 on the North Wilts section. The canal is running alongside the River Thames.
Rear cover, top: The canal near Dauntsey.   *D.G. & B.A. Small*
Rear cover, bottom: In 1998 the canal from Moulden lock to Moredon aqueduct was made fully navigable.   *D.G. & B.A. Small*
Opposite: The River Marden at Calne. Boats locked up from the canal to the wharf which was just beyond the bridge.

Published by The Oakwood Press (Usk), P.O. Box 13, Usk, Mon., NP15 1YS.
E-mail: oakwood-press@dial.pipex.com
Website: www.oakwood-press.dial.pipex.com

Contents

THE WILTS AND BERKS CANAL

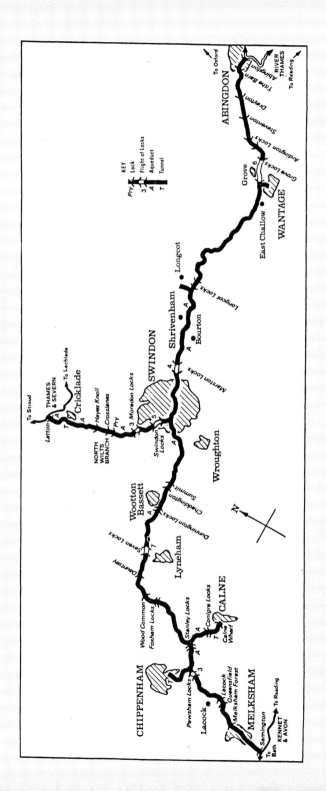

PREFACE TO THE SECOND EDITION

The first edition of this booklet, long out of print, was the result of research work done in the period 1969–71. Since then further details of the early committee and constructional work has come to light in papers found in the former offices of Crowdy's, solicitors of Highworth. Throughout most of the history of the Wilts and Berks canal a Crowdy was the chief clerk of the company. The papers, many in a delicate state, have been pieced together by Dr Bryan Lawton and are now in the hands of the Highworth Historical Society. They were saved from destruction by the prompt action of Mr John Sawyer. In the list of references at the end of the early chapters they are referred to as "The Crowdy letters".

This new information together with the growing interest in the canal fostered by the Wilts and Berks Canal Amenity Group has been the incentive for this second edition incorporating these new facts and bringing up to date the chapter on the present state of the canal remains. The opportunity has been taken to include some photographs newly come to light and a chapter on the day to day routines of the canal Manager as illustrated by a selection of his letters. I make no apology for quoting many documents and letters verbatim as this conveys the spirit of the times more accurately than summaries. I have also quoted financial details in pre-decimal currency; after all the first dividend paid to shareholders was seven shillings per share, not thirty-five pence!

My first canal love was the Kennet and Avon Canal, now rapidly approaching complete restoration, but in 1969 a chance glimpse of "Track of old canal" on the Seventh Series OS map 158 within reasonable distance of my home led me to seek out the remains of the Wilts and Berks north of Wantage, and from this developed two winters of walking the whole length of the canal and its branches and a growing desire to find out the why, when and wherefore.

Swindon Reference Library, Berkshire and Wiltshire Record Offices all yielded up much information, but the best source lay hidden in Gloucestershire Record Office amongst a vast amount of material on the Thames and Severn canal. J.S. Salt, one time Treasurer of that concern was also a shareholder of the Wilts and Berks and amongst his papers there many records remain.

The W&B minute books have been lost. What few books do exist were taken over by Swindon Corporation on abandonment and are preserved in Swindon Reference Library. As the canal was never taken over by a railway Company, few mentions of it exist in the Public Record Office.

This work is the result of this exploration and search for information. It was written for the non-expert and is "the story of" rather than "the history of".

I would like to acknowledge my gratitude to the staffs of Swindon Reference Library, Berkshire, Wiltshire and Gloucestershire Record Offices for their cheerful production of papers etc., to Reg Wilkinson for his photographic labours, to the members of the Wilts and Berks Canal Amenity Group for their contributions and to my wife for her forbearance.

L.J. Dalby, June 1986

A 1793 sketch map of the Canal

Chapter One
The Case for a Canal

At the end of the eighteenth century industry was deserting the south of England in favour of the north and of South Wales where the raw materials for the Industrial Revolution lay close at hand; in its place came the less violent agricultural boom.

At this time the countryside was more densely populated than at present, the community there producing more than enough food for themselves, the surplus being carried away to feed the town and city dwellers, who, in return, sent back manufactured goods. As the living standards of the country communities increased with their greater food production, so also did their demand for building materials and coal to keep them warm; no longer could the countryside provide enough wood for this purpose. The greater use of the land also required coal for lime burning and the facility of moving manure. An efficient transport system was necessary to deal with this diverse flow of commodities.

Those parts of the country lucky enough to be served by navigable rivers used them, the only alternative being the turnpike roads which were at this time unsuitable for heavy or perishable goods. To improve them large quantities of stone were needed; these could most easily be carried by water transport where such existed. Between Chippenham and Calne, two miles from the former, the road ran over marshy ground on a causeway which continually needed repair, a large proportion of its traffic was for its own maintenance.[1]

Wiltshire and west Berkshire, the area later served by the Wilts and Berks, was little served by navigable rivers. The head of the Thames navigation in the eighteenth century was at Lechlade, coal and other goods being distributed from there to neighbouring parts. In the south the River Avon was navigable as far as Bath though proposals had been made to extend the navigation. In 1765 Ferdinando Stratford, engineer, offered to the Worshipful Society of Bristol Merchants a plan and pamphlet proposing short lock cuts between Bath and Melksham bypassing shoals, mills, convolutions etc, and from Melksham to Chippenham a canal parallel to the river. Eleven locks would be necessary and the estimated cost was £15,000.[2] The plan did not lead to any work being undertaken but the proposal did influence the first suggested line of the Kennet and Avon and later that of the Wilts and Berks.

By 1790 Wiltshire was fairly well served by turnpike roads, the principal one being the Bath, Chippenham, Calne, Marlborough route later to become the A4. From Swindon roads led to Faringdon and Oxford, to Cricklade and to Wootton Bassett. From here one branch served Lynham and Calne (B3102) and another Christian Malford and Chippenham (A420). These roads were adequate for pack trains and lightly loaded wagons and were used by Royal Mail coaches averaging seven m.p.h.[1] They were, however, completely unsuited for the conveyance of bulky or heavy loads such as stone for their upkeep, or coal. Further east, the Vale of the White Horse, a rich agricultural area was without an adequate road system. The possibility of water transport here had been surveyed in 1784 first by Robert Whitworth and then by Frederick Page on behalf of the Thames and Severn Canal Company who sought to bypass the upper Thames which they saw as an impediment to their London trade.

Whitworth's survey was for a line from Kempsford on the Thames and Severn to Abingdon, 25 miles long bypassing 46 miles of the river. This would be level for most of its course, descending by 9 locks in the last 5 miles. The plan included a cross link to the river at Hart's Ferry near Newbridge, this would have 4 locks and bypass a large loop, reducing the 24½ miles from the ferry to Abingdon by the river, to 6 miles by the proposed canal.[3] The Page scheme, which would have fulfilled the needs of the Vale more adequately also began at Kempsford but ran further south by way of Highworth and Longcot to Wantage whence one branch ran to Abingdon and one to Wallingford.[4] Both these schemes were defeated in Parliament by Thames and Oxford interests.

In Wiltshire the surveyed northern route of the Western Canal, proposed in 1788 and later to become the Kennet and Avon but on a different line, would have served the upper Avon valley and included Chippenham and Calne. Robert Whitworth, of whom more later, was asked by the canal Committee for his opinion of the survey and also of one for the alternative southern route later chosen by John Rennie. Although Whitworth advised in July 1789 in favour of the latter, with modifications, his earlier proposal for a canal across the Vale of the White Horse and this more recent one checked by him up the Avon valley may well have persuaded him of the possibility, potentiality and advisibility of joining the two together and it is possible that the original idea of the Wilts and Berks canal came from him. The deciding factor was undoubtedly the first suggestion of the Somersetshire Coal Canal early in 1793 which offered the prospect of a plentiful supply of coal for both the K&A and a possible canal up the upper Avon valley and across the Vale of the White Horse to the Thames.

Whether or not Robert was the innovator is only conjecture but the fact that he was soon to be chosen as the engineer for such a waterway may be corroborative evidence.

References

1   History of the County of Wilts.
2   Plan in Wiltshire Record Office.
3   W. Mavor, A general view of the agriculture of Berkshire 1809.
4   T. Rudge, A general view of the agriculture of Gloucester 1807.

Chapter Two
Committee Work 1793–95

The *Bath Chronicle* of 19th July, 1792 contained a mysterious paragraph headed "Canals" which listed the length of all the canals in England at that date. There is no lead in to the paragraph and no conclusions are drawn; one suspects that it was inserted to arouse interest and prepare the ground for either of the proposals soon to appear, for the canal later to become the Somersetshire Coal Canal, or for the Wilts and Berks.

A notice, signed by the Earl of Peterborough whose estate was at Dauntsey, appeared in the same paper on 3rd January, 1793 calling a meeting at Wootton Bassett Town Hall to discuss the promotion of a canal from Abingdon to Bristol or to the intended Western Canal at or near Chippenham. This meeting was held on 30th January with the Earl in the chair. A number of resolutions were passed. It was agreed that the proposed canal "will be of the greatest advantage to the Landed and Commercial interests of this County by opening a regular, safe and certain water carriage between all the towns and places near or adjoining such intended Canal from Bristol to or near Abingdon, and from thence (by means of the Thames) to London." Surveys were to be taken to decide the best line under the direction of the Committee appointed who were given full powers to employ one or more Engineers for the purpose. This Committee consisted of 28 gentlemen, any 5 or more of whom were empowered to meet and act on all matters for carrying the canal into execution.[1]

Of the gentlemen who attended these early meetings and formed the Committee, many were the landowners through whose property the canal was to pass and who hoped that easy transport would improve the value of their holdings, apart from any direct financial gain. Speculators undoubtedly attended, they were prepared to invest large sums in the venture hoping for speedy returns. This was the time of the Canal Mania and there were many examples of canals further north making large profits. The list of shareholders is missing, but when Promissory Notes were issued in 1802 nearly half the money came from London.[2]

The next meeting was held at the Crown and Thistle Inn at Abingdon on 16th February. Robert Whitworth, Brindley's ablest pupil, Engineer of the Forth and Clyde, Surveyor of the Thames and Severn, and with many other canal involvements, together with his son William were appointed to carry out a survey and produce an estimate.

A number of the Committee were at the same time involved in another proposed canal from Bristol to Thames Head on the Thames and Severn which would tap the Gloucestershire coalfield. Whitworth was again appointed to make a survey, he reported that the scheme was impractical and at a meeting on 8th August the idea was dropped. The Abingdon line, however, was luckier, and a meeting of the Committee was called at the Crown Inn, Swindon to hear the Whitworths' report. The minutes of this meeting confirm that at this time the Thames termination had not been settled, it was to be "at or near Abingdon or Wallingford or such other place as may be deemed most expedient." The report was presented by William who apologised that his father was prevented from attending by other engagements; they confirmed that the scheme was practical. A further meeting of the Committee, who would bear the expense of the survey, and the landowners concerned was convened for 29th October to hear further reports. The meeting resolved to take all the necessary steps to apply to Parliament in the ensuing session. By now the decision to use the Western Canal (later the Kennet and Avon) instead of an independent line to Bristol had been taken.

Robert Whitworth's report to the October 1793 meeting on possible water supplies for the summit level was based on a survey taken the previous summer when in the opinion of local millers and others supplies were abnormally low. Even assuming that locks would be of similiar dimensions to those on the Thames and Severn (90 ft long, 12 ft wide, 8½ ft deep) there would be enough water for 28 locks per day. If the reservoir specified in the proposed Act were built no water need be taken from the mills in dry seasons.

He proposed to build the 9½ mile summit 42 ft wide and 7 ft deep utilising the extra 2 ft of depth as a reservoir for 650 lockfuls, enough to absorb the heaviest rains and to store mill water unused at weekends. This extra storage would be enough for one months lockage in dry weather. By utilising also the proposed reservoir, to be called upon during a 2–3 months drought, 20 locks per day could be drawn for 3 months independent of all other sources.

Having examined the summit level Robert delegated the complete survey to his son William with instructions how to proceed. Such was his judgement of the plan and levels drawn that he did not think it necessary to visit the line again.

He then commented on the revision of the line made necessary by the new line of the Kennet and Avon proposed by John Rennie the previous month. The original Western Canal line surveyed first by Weston, Simcock and Barnes in 1788 and later backed by Rennie in 1790 descended from Calne to Chippenham by seven locks, tunnelled 388 yards through the high ground south east of that town and then followed the line of the River Avon, falling by six locks to join the river at Whaddon. From there to Bath seven more locks would be needed on the river to bypass weirs, mills and shoals. From Chippenham to Bath the line followed closely that surveyed by Ferdinando Stratford in 1765 but not taken up at that time. The first proposed W & B line was to join this Western line at or near Chippenham. When Rennie chose instead a more southerly line, incidentally ignoring the Avon and proposing a canal line south of Trowbridge to Bath, Whitworth intended to use the abandoned line from Chippenham to Whaddon, with which he was familiar having been asked to comment on it for the Western Committee in 1789. From Whaddon a 3 mile extension would be necessary to join the K & A south of Trowbridge. To maintain the correct level at the new junction W & B levels would have to be modified as far as Laycock; the lockage on the revised line would be 16 ft less but an additional aqueduct over the River Marden would be needed.

The Bill in preparation would obviously have to be modified; as he thought that there might possibly be an application to make a branch to Malmesbury, both modifications should be included. This is the only mention of such a possible branch.

Whitworth commented that the line of the canal would be easy to build irrespective of whether the eastern termination was at Abingdon or Wallingford. A tunnel some 300 yards long would be necessary to pass under the Street at Chippenham but this was as nothing compared with the 5,000 yard one Rennie proposed on his line. Still assuming that the canal would be built for 90 ft barges, Robert increased his son's estimate for the Abingdon line from £146,000 to £158,000.

When he surveyed the Thames from Abingdon to Wallingford in 1784 he had found it to be a hopeless navigation but since then he had found it vastly improved and recommended that Abingdon be chosen; a line to Wallingford would be 7 miles longer, cost an extra £15,000 and be of no advantage.[3]

The meeting agreed to the Abingdon junction. A select committee was appointed to hold preparatory meetings with both the K&A and T&S to ascertain at what places, and on what terms, junctions with those canals could be made.

Rennie, having changed his line and now not serving Calne and Chippenham directly, proposed to link them with the new line at Foxhangers below Devizes by a 12 mile level branch on the 200 ft contour 8½ miles from Foxhangers a 2 mile branch would leave for Chippenham, the Calne arm joining the River Marden 3½ miles further on. 2 locks on the river would lift boats 18 ft to Calne.[4]

At the next meeting on 12th November a set-back was reported; the K&A had changed their proposed line and rendered the W&B notices incomplete. A subsequent meeting of landowners at Chippenham confirmed that there were other irregularities in the notices, a statement of the probable advantages of the canal and plans thereof had not been published as required by the Rules and Orders of the House of Commons. Thus the intended application to Parliament would have to be postponed. The meeting then resolved that a calculation be made and a report prepared of the commodities which would probably pass on the canal, the quantity and price of the same together with a comparative statement of the expense of land and water carriage. This report is on *page 12*.

James Black, the T&S Engineer, attended this meeting and stated that his Company was in favour of a junction between the two canals and Whitworth was ordered to survey and make an estimate for a link with the T&S at Dudgrove near its junction with the Thames and the W&B at or near Longcot.[6] This survey is missing but is mentioned in letter from E.L. Loveden, a founder subscriber, to Joseph Sills the T&S traffic manager dated 5th October, 1800.

> The Bishop of Durham strongly objects to the line Whitworth projected from Dudgrove as it would make an island of his Beckett Estate. The W&B Committee caused proper notices to be given but have dropped the scheme for this year and intend it should be a distinct measure if ever adopted – I must question if they have ever been in earnest on a Junction, they appeared fond of the plan, perhaps, as a line, to obtain a fresh supply of money and complete their line.

At a meeting in Devizes on 16th January, 1794 the Select Committee reported on a meeting with the K&A on 7th January at Bath. The latter were agreeable to a junction at or near Stanley Farm on their proposed Calne and

WILTS *and* BERKS
C A N A L.

Extract from the Reports of Meffrs. WHITWORTH,
HALL and HUGHES.

THE favourable Report made by Mr. *Whitworth* of the Wilts and Berks Canal,
the abundant Supply of Water without any Injury to Mills, and the vaft Tonnage,
which (according to the Report of Meffrs. *Hall* and *Hughes*) may be expected to
annually pafs thereon, promife great Advantages to the Proprietors, muft be of the
utmoft public Utility and of fingular Service to the Towns and Villages fituated
on the Line. It will open an eafy, cheap, and expeditious Communication betwixt
thofe rich Vales of the White-Horfe and North-Wilts with the two great Marts of
the Kingdom LONDON and BRISTOL ; from which, bad Roads have hitherto in
great Meafure fecluded them. The annual Tonnage reafonably expected to pafs
on this Canal, the above-mentioned Gentlemen (after the moft accurate Inquiry
and Survey that could be made throughout the Line) ftate to be, at leaft 233,644
Tons ; calculating on a moderate Share only of the Briftol and Bath Trade, Carriage of Copper from the Works at Swanfea, to London, Iron from Myrthur and
other Works in that Neighbourhood ; Cheefe throughout the Line for the London
Market ; Salt, Flour, Barley, Malt, Beans, &c. &c.—Building Materials, fuch as
Cornifh and Welfh Tile, Deals, Fir and other Timber ; Bath and Box Stone,
Swindon Stone, Bricks and Lime, Slate, Leather, Wool, Hops, Porter, Cyder,
Glafs and Glafs Bottles, Flints, Lead, Manure, Materials for Highways, &c. &c.

The very material Article of COAL is ftated by the above Gentlemen as follows,
(and this muft be deemed of the moft effential Confequence)—peculiar Attention
was paid to it.

	PRESENT PRICE PER TON.			By this Canal, Coals equal to the Puckle-church, at per Ton.		
	l.	s.	d.	l.	s.	d.
At Abingdon, Sea Coal	2	4	0 }	— 1	1	6
At ditto, by Oxford Canal . . .	1	13	4 }			
At Wantage, Sea Coal	2	5	6 }	—. 1	0	0
At ditto, Staffordfhire Coal . . .	2	5	0 }			
At Shrivenham, Staffordfhire . . .	1	10	0 }	— 0	18	2
At ditto, Pucklechurch . . .	1	16	0 }			
At Swindon	1	16	0	— 0	17	0
At Wootton-Baffett	1	10	0	— 0	16	0
At Chriftian-Malford . . .	1	3	0	— 0	15	0
At Chippenham	1	1	0	—. 0	14	4
At Laycock	1	3	0	— 0	13	10
At Melkfham	1	5	0.	— 0	13	0

HAROLD, PRINTER, MARLBOROUGH,

Chippenham branch and would allow a drawback of 6½ miles, this being the extra distance goods from the W & B would have to travel by first going south on the branch to join the main line and then westward to Bristol etc. The alternative proposal, already anticipated by Whitworth, was that the W & B should carry on the K & A original line to meet the new line south of Trowbridge, in which case the K & A would allow the W & B to build the branches to Calne and Chippenham.[14] It appears that the K & A had no great desire to build their long branch though it would have provided a useful supply of water from the River Marden, a supply later vital to the W & B.

The W & B stood to gain extra trade and reduce their dependence on the K & A so they chose the second alternative and ordered Whitworth to resurvey his line and branches.

The 1794 K & A Act granted them powers to build the long branch but these were to be suspended for 2½ years to enable the W & B to obtain their Act. The subsequent 1795 W & B and 1796 K & A Acts confirmed the change of plan with the proviso that the W & B should connect the two towns to the K & A within 7 years.[7]

The Whitworths' plan was reported to a committee meeting on 2nd February. A completely new line avoided the tunnel at Chippenham by serving that town by a branch rather than the main line. A branch to Calne followed the 200 ft contour on the north side of the Marden to Conigre Farm where two locks lifted it 18 ft to the Calne level. Immediately after the junction with this branch the main line was lowered to the 175 ft contour by the two Stanley locks. The Chippenham branch left the line at Pewsham and ran for 2 miles at this level, 25 ft below Rennie's line necessitating a very deep cutting before Chippenham. The main line was lowered again by the three Pewsham locks and then entered the same Avon valley opposite Lackham House as Rennie's long branch would have used but 55 ft lower down the steep hillside. Three more locks more widely spaced were required to achieve the correct level at Melksham.[8]

The estimate for the main line, including the 3 miles later taken over by the K & A was £103,363, and for the branches, £8,350. Both the survey and estimate were approved.

Subsequently further discussions confirmed that the K & A would agree to the Trowbridge junction, that W & B boats would be allowed to work through to the Somersetshire Coal Canal paying the same tolls as other traffic and that work on the K & A should first commence on the section between Bath and Trowbridge so that it should be ready for traffic from the Coal Canal when the W & B was complete.

A Committee meeting at Wantage on 16th May reaffirmed that the Thames termination should be at Abingdon. A committee was set up to confer with the T & S and the Thames Commissioners on the subject of a possible link between the Thames at Newbridge and the W & B following the earlier suggestion of Robert Whitworth; this link, it will be remembered, would bypass a large convolution in the river.[9] A later meeting at Chippenham on 2nd June was told that the Commissioners would not agree to the link. The meeting then resolved that the Bill should be prepared, the plan and a broadsheet extolling the advantages to be gained from the canal should be published and the consent of landowners and occupiers sought.

At the August meeting William Whitworth reported that he understood that the Coal Canal was to accommodate boats carrying 25 tons only which size was considered the most beneficial to the Proprietors and useful to the community. He therefore advised that the W&B should be a narrow canal costing only two thirds of one for 50 ton barges.[10] The canal was built 27 ft wide at the surface, 14 ft wide at the bottom and 4½ ft deep.[11]

He also reported that the K&A had had another change of mind and now intended to join the W&B at Semington 4 miles short of the earlier intended point; they had abandoned the loop round Trowbridge and were to use 4 miles already surveyed for the W&B which would thus be saved the expense (£9,000) of building that length. The K&A paid £174.3.0 to cover the cost of the survey.[12] This change was also incorporated in the draft Bill.

Once the plans were published many objections were raised by people who saw threats, real and imaginary, to their lands and property. For example, Lord Carnarvon wrote to the Earl of Peterborough on behalf of a farmer tenant who claimed that a stream across Christian Malford Common was essential to the prosperity of his farm; a clause was inserted in the Bill forbidding the Company to interfere with this stream.[14] Many other rights and properties were similarly protected; in some cases permission to cross certain lands was only granted if certain provisos were included.

The route chosen for the canal passed through no towns, and in fact the only settlements developing large enough to envelop it during its active life were Swindon and Melksham; at the time of building the former was a mere village of 1,198 souls lying a mile south of the line. The populations of other towns nearby were in 1801,

Melksham 5,006	Calne 3,767	Wantage 2,339
Chippenham 3,366	Wootton Bassett 1,244	Abingdon 4,356

Abingdon was already well supplied by the Thames and the Oxford canal but would provide an outlet to the river for coal and an alternative route to London. Lyneham, perched on a hilltop, was separated from the canal by 2 miles of steep road, the wharf at Dauntsey being built to serve its trade. Shrivenham, Uffington, the Challows and Grove were tiny villages, in fact from Swindon to Abingdon the line passed through sparsely populated country, Wantage being the only town of any size nearby.

On 6th February, 1795 leave was sought to introduce a Bill for "The Abingdon and Trowbridge Canal". The Petitioners stated that the canal would:

> greatly facilitate the Conveyance of Corn, Coal, Stone, Iron, Timber, Lime, Chalk, Manure and all kinds of merchandise and heavy commodities, not only to and from Bath and the several towns of Trowbridge, Melksham, Chippenham, Calne, Wootton Bassett, Swindon, Highworth, Faringdon, Wantage, Abingdon, Wallingford and other adjacent towns, but also to and from the ports of London and Bristol.

The petition was referred to a Committee under Charles Dundas who besides sheperding canal bills through Parliament was also the Chairman of the K&A Company. In support William Whitworth stated that he had lately taken levels and surveys and had found the line suggested practical. The Rector of Uffington, the Reverend George Watts and Edward Thornhill of

Kingston Lisle gave evidence that the canal would be of great benefit to the area. Only Oxford, claiming that the canal would be harmful to the city's trade, petitioned against, unsuccessfully. The Bill passed smoothly and on 30th April, 1795 received the Royal assent.[13]

The cost of preparing and steering the Act through Parliament was £5,796.13.10. The Select Committee on the Bill had met on 20th February, 1795 at Alice's Coffee House in the House of Commons and made a call of £2 per subscriber "as the expense of soliciting the Act is very considerable". This was the second call, £1 per share had been made previously. Calls of £5 were made on the shares at approximately three monthly intervals up to the final one in December 1800.

The ten members from the Wiltshire and Berkshire districts met on 4th June, 1796 to elect five others as stipulated in the Act. William Hallett was elected Chairman of the Company, John Ralph the Principal Clerk. The Treasurer was James Montagu, replaced later in the year by Matthew Humphries. Ambrose Goddard, Lord of the Manor of Swindon was elected Chairman of the Committee of Management.

Footnote: Engraved plan by Whitworths dated 1793 is to be found as a pullout at the back of this book.

References

1   The report of this and subsequent meetings appeared in the *Bath Chronicle.*
2   SRL List of Promissory note holders.
3   CL 1.
4   First 1793 K & A engraved plan.
5   CL 2.
6   GCL FF 14 54.
7   Western Canal Minute Book, PRO Kew.
8   SRLG 998.
9   W. Mavor. A general view of the agriculture of Berkshire 1809.
10   CL 3.
11   Account of the rivers and canals west of London, Zachary Allnutt 1810.
12   K & A account book.
13   JHC Vol 50 p157 – 432.
14   WRO 109/900/910.
CL   Crowdy letters.
GCL   Gloucester City Library.
JHC   Journal of the House of Commons.
PRO   Public Record Office.
SRL   Swindon Reference Library.
SRLG   Swindon Reference Library, Goddard papers.
WRO   Wiltshire Record Office.

Wilts and Berks Canal.

In Purſuance of an Act of Parliament paſſed in the 35th Year of the Reign of his Majeſty King GEORGE the Third, intituled

" An Act for making and maintaining a Navigable Ca-
" nal from the River THAMES, or ISIS, at or near the
" Town of Abingdon, in the County of Berks, to join
" or communicate with the Kennet and Avon Canal,
" at or near the Town of Trowbridge, in the County
" of Wilts, and alſo certain Navigable Cuts therein
" deſcribed."

This Ticket certifies that *Ambroſe Goddard*, is a Proprietor of this Undertaking, and intitled to a Share therein numbered *236*,

In Teſtimony whereof the Common Seal of the Company is hereunto affixed this *1ſt December* in the Year of our Lord One Thouſand Seven Hundred and *ninety five*

A Share Certificate.

Chapter Three
The Years of Construction, 1795–1810

The purchase of lands commenced immediately the Act became law; this did not always proceed either legally or smoothly. T. Bruges, an agent at Melksham, writes on 19th December, 1795 that he could not get Mr Long to sign a conveyance and told how "when the Gentlemen of the Coal Canal Committee wanted to see him, they took the opportunity of shewing the plan just as he was getting into his carriage." At the end of the same month he writes "Mr Long, being old, and Mrs Thresher, being ill, still refuse to sign for strangers" and requests that Mr Ralph deal with the matter himself. He complains also that Mrs Thresher's land had been entered by workmen before everything had "been adjusted".[1] James Johnson writes on 27th January, 1796 that he had just been informed that Canal Company workmen had entered his premises and begun to dig for clay; this surprised him as Mr Whitworth had assured him that he should first be consulted and the price of the land agreed if not actually paid over.

Records were kept of all land conveyances in a book of 45 large scale (20 inches to the mile) plans still to be seen in Swindon Reference Library. Those for the branches are missing; the Canal Manager later stated that no such plan of the Calne branch had ever been made. Similar plans were later drawn of the North Wilts canal.

A 1795 Whitworth report[2] stated that the line had been marked out as far as Forest Gate (the present A4 crossing at Pewsham) which included six locks each with a 9ft rise. As the canal could not be used until locks and bridges were complete the production of bricks for these should have priority over level cutting. Clay should be dug and bricks baked as close as possible to where they were required. They should be 10in. long, 4¾in. wide and 3in. deep, 700 being equal in volume to 1000 common statute bricks. This would save expense and incur less duty.

Two major culverts would be required, one 110ft long under the 18ft embankment over Labburns Brook in Melksham and one 84ft under the 12ft embankment over Forest Brook near Bessel's Farm. Each would be 5ft high and 6ft wide, sufficient to cope with flood water. These had to be built before embanking could be started. The buried parts could be built with rough stone but as he wished everything about the canal to look handsome the facings should be of Box Ashlar.

Kimmeridge clay suitable for bricks was plentiful all along the line. The first brickyards were built at Melksham followed by others at Pewsham, Stanley, at Conigre Farm on the Calne branch, at Foxham, Dauntsey, Trow Lane, Dunnington below Wootton Bassett, Marston and Longcot, the last bricks baked at each yard being used to build the kilns of the next. On 28th November, 1795 *Jackson's Oxford Journal* reported that 4 million bricks would be needed between Melksham and Calne.

Stephen Holland and John Bosville and their labourers excavated the three miles northward from Semington and prepared the foundation pits for eight arch and four lift bridges in this section. John Smith and John Bosville were responsible for the bricklaying and masonry work including the bridge over the Melksham – Calne Turnpike which had to be of stone as no bricks were ready when needed.

Robert Whitworth (Senior) in a report dated 23rd June, 1797[3] pointed out that it was essential to build a regulating lock at Semington to protect the 3 mile level to Melksham Forest lock and also to allow the length to be drained for maintenance.

> The K & A towpath must be carried over the tail of the lock by a bridge. Apart from a 100 yard length preserved to bank up the Turnpike Road bridge over the K & A when it is built the W & B is almost complete to the Turnpike Road Bridge at Melksham, itself complete. The embankment in Melksham must be raised another 2 ft to give the required 4½ ft depth of water. The necessary earth cannot be moved until the boats presently in use at Queensfield can be freed. Everything is ready for the building of Melksham Forest lock; from here to Stroud the canal is nearly finished, Queensfield lock complete and Laycock lock under way. From Stroud to the bottom Pewsham lock, apart from slips in the high ground (opposite Lackham House) the canal is nearly finished. The bottom lock is complete except for the coping stones which must be brought by water, the middle one is nearly complete but the top one not yet started. The swivel bridge [sic] over the entrance to the Chippenham branch and the substantial 24 ft wide Turnpike Road [now the A4] Bridge at Forest Gate is finished. From here to Stanley much digging and boating will be needed. the aqueduct over the Calne River (Marden) of two 12 ft arches is set out and should be completed by the end of Summer. Stanley bottom lock is being built and the digging from here to Foxham nearly complete. The branch to Calne is progressing. There is bad slippery ground above Hazeland Mill and much puddling will be necessary. Two locks will be needed to lift the canal to the Calne level. The crossing of the Turnpike road [A4] near Studleybridge will not be easy to accomplish. The branch to Chippenham is almost finished. By early Spring the canal will be complete from the K & A to Chippenham, to within 1½ miles of Calne and up to Foxham, 15½ miles supplied from the Marden at Conigre Farm. As we have some very good undertakers at work please issue orders to keep them working, we must not lose them.

Who were these "good undertakers"? Smith and Bosville worked north from Forest Brook while William Edwards was working south from the Pewsham locks to meet them. He encountered many slips in the steep ground mentioned by Whitworth, this section included an abnormal number of culverts and much piling. Edwards also built the Stanley aqueduct foundations and the new river course, boating 4,425 cu. yds of spoil from the deep cutting near Stanley to embank the valley crossed by the aqueduct and 3,700 cu. yds from Pewsham Top to back up the locks and basins below. Taking advantage of a kink in the river course, the aqueduct was built on dry land on the west side, the river then being diverted under it and the previous course filled in to form the eastern approach. 123,000 bricks and 32½ tons of timber for staging were used.

William Large was responsible for the wood work in this section. During 1796 he submitted an account for 8 drawbridges between Foxham and Stanley, 6 between Melksham and Stanley, 3 between Foxham and Dauntsey, 2 on the Chippenham branch and 7 on the Calne line, all charged at £4.10s.0d each. he also built 6 boats of elm 40 ft long at £5.5s.0d each, 2 of oak 70 ft long at £12.12s.0d each and another of oak 70 ft long with a cabin, deck etc. for use by the Committee. He supplied all the lock gates between Melksham and Foxham and on the Calne branch, these being made and hung for £12.12s.0d per set.

The 1797 Committee progress report précised the Whitworths' report and added

> The Committee are desirous of having that part of the canal between the junction with the K&A and Foxham completed before they proceed further, as the saving of expense in the carriage of stone and other materials in boats instead of land carriage to the works above will be very considerable. And when the Coal Canal and that part of the K&A which lies between the Coal Canal and Semington is opened the carriage of coal may be expected to produce an interest on the money expended, as the towns of Melksham, Calne and Chippenham and the country adjacent will be by that means supplied therewith.[4]

But this was not to be. Avoncliff and Biss aqueducts on the K&A, vital links in the chain, were not completed until late 1798 and then Dundas aqueduct was unfinished. Work then recommenced on the northern section of the W&B line.

The southern brickyards were still at work. In 1797 John Heath produced 300,000 bricks at Conigre Farm, 110,000 at Foxham, 206,000 at Pewsham. In 1798 Conigre Farm produced 354,000, Pewsham 196,000 and Foxham 400,000. A new yard was opened at Dauntsey baking 200,000 that year, Pewsham yard levelled and later that at Conigre Farm was cleared and the clay pits filled by John Gale. The average lift bridge used 15,000 bricks, arch bridges 35,000 while a typical lock consumed 178,000 and 425 cu. ft of stone. A lock with a tail bridge required 206,000 and the three deep Pewsham locks 630,000 in all.

Robert Whitworth's 13th January, 1798 report[5] stated that 16 miles of the canal were complete at a cost of £33,000. He suggested that a basin and wharf for coals be built at Dauntsey; while it was not at present necessary to build the lock and bridge or cut the deep ground up to the Turnpike road (A420) it would be necessary to cut the canal up to Bowd's Farm to provide a reservoir to collect and retain water to supply the lockage to bring up coals, the 1½ miles containing some 100 lockfuls. The remaining 1½ miles of the Calne branch would include two 8 ft locks at Conigre Farm and be easy to build except for the obstacle of the stony hill at Studley-bridge. Tests would be necessary; if the ground at the bottom of the hill was running sand, clay or marl then the best plan would be to cut straight through the hill either in a cutting or, if the sides were unstable, a 100 yard tunnel. The hill should provide a large quantity of rubble stone for towpath and possibly some rock for less important copings. The tunnel would be easy to build by a cut and cover method, replacing the soil but boating away the stone.

The test results were in favour of the tunnel which was duly built.

It will be remembered that as a result of changes in levels the Chippenham branch was at a low level and first terminated in England's Meadow with high ground ahead. About this time Chippenham Council pointed out that the Act specified the termination to be within 100 yards of the town. They complained that whereas Chippenham consisted of upwards of 500 houses, within 100 yards of the proposed terminus there were only 15 small houses and so the Company had not complied with the Act. Whitworth was asked for a scheme to get around this objection and produced estimates on 23rd August 1798. He costed two alternatives, the canal terminating either in the garden opposite the wide part of Timber Street or in the meadow called the Bulls Hill. The former would involve 540 yards of very deep cutting, destroy 3 acres of garden and cost £1,500. The Bulls Hill alternative would involve only 400 yards of level cutting and cost only £327.[6]

The adopted solution was to build a 90 yard tunnel under John Simpkin's garden which, together with the wharf was built in 1800 by Thomas Phillips. The termination was specified absolutely in the 1801 Act as "In or near the site of a dwelling house and garden belonging to Ralph Hale Gaby". On 30th June, 1801 the Council decreed that all trading bargemasters should pay them two shillings for each barge, the wharf being evermore a private one.[7]

In 1797/8 Clark and Thatcher excavated from Stanley Top to the road at Bremhill Wick. In the same period John and Thomas Nock built Stanley Top, nine arch and nine lift bridges and 7 ft diameter, 75 ft long culvert passing Cadenham Brook under the canal. Hunter provided a lead pipe to carry water to Laycock Abbey across the canal bed. The gap between the southern end of the line and the K & A was cut in 1799 by Holland, John Ash excavated the regulating lock pit at Semington and Thomas Thatcher cut the entrance into the K & A. James McIlquham, who was also responsible for the Dundas and Avoncliff aqueducts on the K & A, built the lock, the masonry towpath bridge over the tail and the abutting walls involving 5,545 cu. yds of stone.

In 1798 John Wilkins surveyed the section between Foxham and Bowd's Farm, this 3½ mile stretch being excavated by John Clark in 1798/9. By now the Foxham and Dauntsey brickyards were being left behind, the former producing 1,237,000 in 1799 and the latter 55,000, both yards being cleared in 1800. With the prospect of seven locks and numerous bridges ahead a new yard was built at Trow Lane, Tockenham, the bricks for the kilns being boated from Dauntsey. The new yard baked 732,000 in 1799 and 741,000 in 1801.

The 20th December, 1798 report of Robert Whitworth[8] is the last one bearing his signature. He died in 1799, all subsequent progress reports being signed either by William, his son, or William Hallett the W & B Chairman. Robert reported that the regulating lock was being built, the 8 locks to Foxham finished except for coping stones some of which would be carried by water from the Calne branch tunnel. Also completed were 23 arch bridges, 18 swivel, Stanley aqueduct, 16 large culverts and 19 smaller ones. The steep ground opposite Lackham was still troublesome, more piling was necessary. One lock at Foxham was half built, the lock pit and arched bridge ready at Christian Malford Common. Two thirds of the digging between Foxham and Dauntsey was finished, the branch to Chippenham completed as also was the Calne branch to the proposed basin in Patford Meadow except for the tunnel and the Conigre lock gates. A dangerous slip in the Marquis of Lansdown's wood would require strong piling, also another above Hazeland Mill needed securing with large blocks of stone from the tunnel, earlier attempts using brick having been crushed and brushed aside by the sliding of the ground above. He had surveyed the extension proposed by the Marquis from the basin in Patford Meadow up to the town mill. Although the distance was only 300 yards, a lock with a 5 ft rise, culverts and sluices would be necessary, costing £970. By not having to build a road to Patford Meadow £300 would be saved. 34 yards of the tunnel had been arched but work had ceased until the Spring as water tended to wash the cutting away before the side walls could be built and the arch turned.

In the 1798/9 period William Large took down and rebuilt one side of both Stanley and Pewsham Top locks, built the lock at Christian Malford Common (Wood Common) and supplied two more boats, one 40 ft and the other 25 ft long. Most of the woodwork supplied by Large was produced at the carpenters shop at Stroud, demolished in 1799. John Smith and John Bosville were still busy at this time pointing locks and bridges, excavating Dauntsey lock pit and the foundation pits for 6 waste weirs at various sites.

The first suspicion that his father's estimate of the canal's water supplies might have been too generous came in William Whitworth's report of 13th May, 1799.[9] While he thought that the streams the Company were empowered to tap for nine months of the year would suffice, he had marked out a reservoir in the valley above Trow Lane (later Tockenham) about 400 yards from the canal. With 9 acres surface area and 8½ ft of depth this could hold 514 locks, or if the head was raised another 5 ft, double that quantity. He pointed out that a deep cutting would be required at Trow Lane, the earth from which would be needed to embank a deep valley a ½ mile on at Tockenham Wick. The cheapest and most convenient way to carry this would be in boats and as this would be a slow job the work should commence some time before the contract for the next locks was let ensuring that the necessary stone and coal be brought by water. He estimated that the nearly 3 miles from Bowd's Farm to the Turnpike road near Hunt Mill (A420) together with the lock bridge and deep cutting at Dauntsey would cost £10,200.

On 6th June, 1800[10] he reported that the canal was navigable to Dauntsey where work was nearing completion extending the line to Bowd's Farm, 21 miles in all. Work on the Chippenham and Calne branches had been suspended pending an Act to cover the amended terminations. The embankment below Tockenham house still required some months work before the canal reached Hunts Mill.

This report acknowledged that to date the cost had exceeded the estimates by some £17,500. The slips on the Calne branch and the cutting and tunnel made necessary there due to the bad ground at Studleybridge, the increased cost of the Tockenham embankment, the possible shortage of water making it expedient to build 7 instead of 6 locks at Trow Lane, and the increasing cost of land all contributed to the overspend. In addition there had been a 20% increase in labour costs, the additional duty on bricks and the fact that owing to the unfinished state of the K & A and the Coal Canal all coal, stone and lime had to be carried on land. No difficulties were foreseen between Hunt's Mill and Abingdon and it was considered this line should be completed within 2 years.[11]

In 1802 Brown and McIlquham built the seven locks, one below and six above Bowd's Bridge, each consuming 500 cu. yds of brick and 350 cu. yds of stone for "parapets, hollow posts, trunks and square quoins." The locks were spaced about 100 yards apart, the contractors cutting all the pits, the wide pounds between, and wheeling all the spoil for banking etc. Their bill was £5,218. The same year Edwards and Cam excavated the mile from the east side of Tockenham valley to the road near Hunt's Mill, some of the spoil being boated to Tockenham valley, some wheeled to the valley below Vastern and some to raise the road at Passon's Bridge.

From now on progress reports were signed by the Committee of Management rather than by the Engineer. That of 25th November, 1802[12] stated that the Calne branch was finished and a wharf erected. The Chippenham tunnel was complete and a considerable length of very deep cutting in a state of forwardness. The navigation was open to Wootton Bassett between which place and Swindon several miles had been cut and many bridges built. Only four more locks were needed to reach the east end of the summit at South Marston; the bricks were ready and this part of the line would be open next year when the extent of the navigation would be 34 miles. The Toll Collectors house at Semington and other lockhouses were built. The Committee expressed their satisfaction with the manner in which the work has been planned and executed by Mr Whitworth. The cost to date was £93,000.

The demand for bricks was never ending. In 1802 James Dobson baked 245,000 at Trow Lane and also built a new yard at Dunnington below Wootton Bassett producing 1,173,000 that year and 406,000 in 1803. Edwards and Camm completed the work in the Tockenham area, wheeling and boating bricks from Trow Lane to various culverts and bridges, carting 181,000 for the aqueduct over Wootton Bassett Brook and for the bridges between the Dunnington locks and at the Marlborough road. They also excavated the ½ mile between Vastern wharf and the west side of the brook valley, using the spoil to build up the embankment across the valley, and finally, nearly 2 miles from the embankment to the start of the summit level on Chaddington Common.

In 1803 William Quarrel built the four remaining locks to the summit, two at Dunnington and one each at Chaddington and Summit. Henry Holland built the masonry bridge at Chaddington Common, and some miles further on David Burrel built the aqueduct with two 6 ft arches over Wroughton Brook. The level section between Summit lock and Swindon Wharf was excavated from both ends in 1804, Thomas King working up to Hay Lane and Gregor McGregor from Swindon. The canal ran one mile north of Swindon, the summit water supply being drawn from Wroughton Brook through a feeder from Deacon's Mill. The ¼ mile above this feeder passed through an area known as Rushey Platt which presented a real challenge. Britton in his *Topographical Sketches of North Wiltshire 1826* describes it as "an area of quagmires which are considered to be of great depth and consequently shunned as places of danger." Dr William Smith, the geologist and one time surveyor of the Coal Canal was consulted by the W & B on how to carry the canal through the moving bog "unhealthy and plagued". The crossing involved serious engineering difficulties and Smith was a frequent visitor to Swindon.

By 31st March, 1804 boats were using the canal to Swindon Wharf, the bricks used in the warehouse there being boated from Trow Lane, probably the last that yard produced. The Company erected a row of houses west of the wharf on the north bank, these being known as Cetus Buildings, Cetus being the Latin for whale. The Whale Public House and Whale Bridge were adjacent. The buildings were to house the workmen who constructed and maintained the canal.

In 1804 also James Johnson built a brickyard at Marston producing 1,559,000 bricks that year and 764,000 in 1805. Gregor McGregor excavated the section from Swindon Wharf to Marston Top lock. An isolated section from the Marlborough–Shrivenham road to Longcot Top lock had already been cut by Thomas King in 1803 together with the aqueduct pit at Beckett Brook and the new brook courses at each end. Edwards and Camm completed the linking section, dug the foundations of the four Marston locks, cut the aqueduct pit and the new river course at Acorn Bridge and adjusted the bank at the head of the Wanborough Brook feeder. William Quarrel built the Marston locks, two with tail bridges, the aqueduct at Acorn Bridge with three 7 ft arches over the river Cole and that with the single 7 ft arch at Beckett.

The 21st June, 1805 report[13] stated that the canal had been navigable for some time to the east end of the summit at South Marston and that a convenient wharf had been made at Swindon. Two of the four locks planned at Marston and the aqueduct at Acorn Bridge had been built and the greater part of the earth work, bridges and all the culverts were finished to Longcot; the canal would be open to there in November, 39 miles were already completed. £56,000 was the estimate for completion to Abingdon.

The overrun in cost was again attributed to the expense of the Act, wharves, warehouses, weighing machines, Committee, Engineers and Agents, compensation paid to millers, purchase of mills and of land which the Company had been obliged to take when required to do so by the owners in consequence of being divided into small pieces. The interest paid to Proprietors up to September 1800 and to the Treasurer in advance, the extension of the branches into Calne and Chippenham and the tunnels and deep cuttings necessary, variations in line for several mills not allowed for in the original estimates, increase of brick duty and the great advances in the price of land, materials and wages were further reasons for the additional costs.

Longcot was reached on 29th November, 1805, the new sections being filled by temporary feeders from Bishopstone and Wanborough brooks. That year John Jobson built the last and biggest brickworks of all at Longcot producing 380,000 bricks, 927,000 in 1806, 1,165,000 in 1807, 2,199,000 in 1808 and 1,225,000 in 1809, these like all the others being perfectly plain with no bonding recess. Map No. 31 in the plan book contains a note concerning the drains marked below Longcot Top lock; "The covered hollow drain in field 309 was made by the Company. There is also another covered drain on the south side of the canal. These were made and the ground filled up, where brick clay had been dug by the Company so that no more damage will be claimed from them."

In 1805 the Company fleet was increased to 25, William Large supplying three earth boats 40 ft long for £24 each and a 30 ft Committee boat.

The 6th June, 1807 progress report[14] states that the canal was now complete to Challow, making, with the branches, 49 miles. One mile beyond was in an advanced state leaving only 8½ miles to reach Abingdon, exclusive of the ¾ mile Wantage branch delayed only by the very exorbitant demands of the land owners. The ¾ mile branch at Longcot, not previously allowed for, had been built to extend the trade to the north of the canal. The undertaking had suffered considerably by an unavoidable delay in settling the new branch, by the bad state of the road to Longcot and by the K&A not supplying their locks with water at Bath to effect a communication with Bristol.

George Roe of Challow completed the line but his records lack detail to date the various works. Between Longcot and Abingdon there were 27 draw-bridges, 10 arch bridges, an aqueduct over Letcombe Brook and 6 locks at Grove, 2 at Ardington and singles at Steventon, Drayton, Tythe Barn and Abingdon. On 24th February, 1809 Thomas Rogers was paid £4.10s.0d for 6 weeks lock keeping at Grove before the locks were open for trade. Later George Roe was one of the contractors for the Stratford and Moreton tramway.

The Thames was reached officially on 10th September, 1810. The event was described in *The Morning Chronicle* of 19th September.

> The opening of the Wilts and Berks canal into the River Thames, at Abingdon, was celebrated there on Friday last, with every demonstration of joy. At half past two o'clock, a body of the Proprietors, in the Company's boat, with music playing passed the last lock into the Thames, amidst the loud huzzas of a large concourse of people, who lined the sides of the Canal. The party proceeded from the banks of the Thames to the Council Chamber, where they were joined by the Members of Parliament for Cricklade, Abingdon, Oxford, Hereford, Ludgershall &c. &c. and many Gentlemen of the neighbourhood, and partook of an excellent dinner prepared for the occasion. Wm. Hallett, Esq. the Chairman, prefaced his toast of "Success to the Wilts and Berks Canal", with a concise speech, in which he stated, that the concern was in such high credit, that every Proprietor who regularly proceeded on his original Subscription, could, at the present price of shares, obtain cent. per cent. upon his capital (an advantage, at so early a period, unprecedented in the history of Canals), and commented with great ability on the future prospects of the undertaking. His address was received with every mark of satisfaction, and the Proprietors, in bursts of applause, expressed how sensibly they felt their obligations to him for his many years persevering exertions as Chairman of the Committee of Management, and unanimously resolved that their thanks for his services should be presented to him, engraven on a piece of plate to the value of 100 guineas. The day was spent with great conviviality and harmony, enlivened by many appropriate toasts and songs, until the company, highly gratified, separated at a late hour.

Whitworth's last known report, dated 5th April, 1811 stated

> The works that remain to be completed are, the raising of the banks of the canal between the two locks at Abingdon, about a mile of towpath and some fencing and also the coping and guarding of some of the locks on the main line, the whole of the towing path and fencing, one or two bridges and a little earth work on the branch to Wantage. Another bridge over the River Ock and the wharf to be completed and warehouse to be erected at Abingdon, and if necessary at Wantage also. The expense of these works, the settling of the Contractors, Landowners and Occupiers accounts and the expenses of the feeder now making I cannot accurately state, but I conceive may amount to about £10,000.

The total cost of the completed work was £255,262.10s.9½d.

References

Details of construction from Superintendents ledgers A&B SRL

1	WRO 109/900/910.	6	CL 7.	11	BRO D EEL 07 bundle 1.
2	CL 4.	7	Records of Chippenham SRL.	12	CL 22, SRLG 1004.
3	CL 5, SRLG 999.	8	CL 8.	13	CL 29, SRLG 1008.
4	SRLG.	9	CL 9.	14	CL 30.
5	CL 6.	10	CL 14.		BRO Berkshire Record Office.

Chapter Four

Committee Business 1800–1817

Early in 1800 two parties of disgruntled Proprietors caused the Company to seek legal advice.[1] The first pointed out that between February 1794 and the present £89 had been called on each £100 share. This, together with the accumulated interest of 5% as specified by the 1795 Act, brought the total to £101.2s.1d and therefore the Company had no right to make extra calls as they proposed to do. The advice of V. Gibbs of Lincoln's Inn was that the interest should not be considered as money actually paid so further calls would be in order.

The second complaint came from shareholders in Chippenham who pointed out that the Company had not complied with the Act by terminating their branch within some 100 yards of cottages in Wood Lane. Chippenham was an ancient Borough with Bailiffs, Burgesses and Freemen for the time being living in Freehouses and the complainants wanted the termination within 100 yards of the nearest Freehouse in the orchard opposite giving a good straight road to the Market Place. The road to Wood Lane was very narrow and crooked, unsuitable for the carriage of heavy goods. Legal advice again supported the Company but as we have already seen in the previous chapter they gave way.

In July 1800 seven Proprietors, including William Hallett their Chairman, went on a tour of inspection of their own line and also the K&A and SCC the progress of which was of vital concern to the W&B. They reported to Ambrose Goddard, the Chairman of the Committee of Management on 28th July.[2]

They had examined the line from Tockenham to Semington, including the branches and were completely satisfied with what they found, praising Whitworth's efforts. The only work to be completed, apart from some towpaths, was the coping of the brickwork of some bridges, the stone for which would be carried by water from Bradford when the K&A was navigable.

They also examined the K&A line from Semington to the SCC finding that the progress and work on that part of the line, so important to the interests of the W&B "are not such as might have been expected from the Terms and Nature of their Undertaking to complete the same, and from the repeated assurances of several respectable persons concerned therein." However Whitworth's opinion supported by their own observations and the assurance of Mr Clarke, the K&A engineer, was that navigation of the vital section would be possible in 3–4 months.

The link between the SCC and Bath was in a more advanced state, this too would be of the utmost consequence, affording a communication between the W&B and the cities of Bath and Bristol. At Limpley Stoke the party was joined by Mr Stevens the Proprietor of the Camerton Colliery and senior representatives of the SCC who accompanied them to Bath discussing on the way the state of that canal and the coal trade. The following day the W&B and SCC party visited Coombe Hay where a difference in level of 154ft was to be negotiated by an inclined plane, the earlier ill fated Cassion Lock having been abandoned.[3] The Dunkerton line to the upper level was complete and

25

the 4½ miles from the lower to the K&A almost so, Mr Bennet, the SCC Engineer assuring them that it would be navigable in about 3 months
Camerton coal, of excellent quality would cost ten shillings at the Pit. At the foot of the unfinished works at Coombe Hay the price would have risen to twelve shillings and nine pence and at Semington to fifteen shillings when both the SCC and K&A were open.

By early 1801 the Company was in financial trouble. Of the 1,119 £100 shares allowed by the Act only 666 had been subscribed and £61,512 in cash collected, all this and also £3,797 advanced by the Treasurer Matthew Humphries had been spent and various other debts incurred. They could not under their present powers raise further funds until the original subscription had been filled so an application was made to Parliament on 16th February, 1801 for powers to raise a further £200,000. At the same time powers to make additions and modifications to the earlier Act were requested. The resulting Act 41 Geo. 111 Cap. 68 received the Royal Assent on 20th June, 1801 and gave the Company powers to raise £200,000 over and above the original £111,900 by creating new shares of £100 at the rate of £60 per share or at any other value declared, the purchasers to have all the advantages of the original Proprietors. Money already lent to the Company or owing on lands could be used to purchase shares and 5% per annum discount would be allowed on money advanced on shares before being called.If the whole £200,000 could not be raised in this way Promissory notes of not less than £50 each could be issued, these were to be payable after 10 years either in cash or in stock of the Company. Interest on these notes was to be paid in preference to dividends.

The Company were finding the clause in the original Act concerning the payment of 5% interest on money subscribed until the canal be completed an undesirable burden, they had paid out £6,925 as such interest already. The new Act repealed this clause, no interest was to be paid after 29th September, 1800.

It had also been found inconvenient to require the shutting and fastening of swivel and drawbridges, instead the Company was to provide a chain extending across the bottom of the canal to enable persons to shut them if necessary.

Finally the agreement with the K&A on the junction at Semington was confirmed, also the termination at Chippenham in or near the site of a dwelling house and gardens belonging to Ralph Hale Gaby, and in Calne at or near the pound or dam of Town Mill belonging to the Marquis of Landsdowne.

In June 1801 subscribers for a survey of a proposed canal from Abingdon to Aylesbury, very probably W&B interests, heard William Whitworth's report.[4] He had found a line from Aylesbury, easy to execute, locking down some 91 ft to the Thames on the lower side of Culham Bridge. Obviously the Thames navigation between Culham and Abingdon held more fears for him than it had earlier for his father for he suggested that a better plan would be to cross the river by an aqueduct high enough to allow barges to pass underneath. This would require a long and high embankment from the aqueduct to a junction with the W&B near the Abingdon–Drayton road. Water would be supplied from the Grand Junction Aylesbury branch supplemented either from the River Thame or one or two reservoirs.

The scheme progressed no further at that time as the Grand Junction, probably fearing embarrassing demands for water, would not countenance the building of their Aylesbury branch, authorised in 1794 and so vital to the plan. It was revived as the Western Junction Canal 8 years later when the Marquis of Buckingham and others only agreed to withdraw their opposition to the Grand Union Bill if the GJ built the branch.

Following the 1801 Act a meeting at the Crown Inn, Swindon on 16th July, 1801 resolved that 1,400 new and additional shares of £100 each should be created. Of them, 666, the same number as shares held by the present Proprietors would be at £60 per share, the value of the remainder to be fixed at future special meetings. The preference offered to the original shareholders should be taken up in writing within 6 weeks.[5]

The inclined plane on the SCC was not a success and the Committee then planned to substitute conventional locks on both lines of the canal. An Act would be necessary to raise sufficient money to complete the canal and at the same time seek permission to levy an extra toll of one shilling per ton on coal passing the locks. This aroused considerable opposition from both the W&B and K&A who pointed out that their original Acts allowed them a toll of 3½d per ton per mile on coal, and the SCC 2½d. As the W&Bs main object was the carriage of coal their calculations were based on these figures and they had quoted prices to the public which they would not be able to honour if the SCC continued in its present imperfect state or were allowed to take an additional toll if improved by the building of locks. The SCC should build the locks by defraying the expense themselves. Both the K&A and W&B are raising additional sums to complete their canals without demanding additional tonnage. The preamble to the SCC Act specified a canal fit for 50 ton barges and with locks. Instead it was made narrow and the Company who substituted an inclined plane now wishes to make the public pay for correcting their mistake.[6]

Despite this joint protest a compromise was reached in March 1802 and a SCC act of 30th April approved the substitution of locks. A Lock Fund of £45,000 was formed to join the Dunkerton and Radstock branches to the lower level. The K&A, the W&B and the SCC each contributed £15,000. The Fund charged one shilling per ton on coal while the SCC charged 2½d per ton mile of which ¾d was payable to the Fund. The three subscribers were limited to 10 per cent per annum on their capital, the surplus being used for paying off the capital, and when this was paid off the extra lock tonnage was to cease.[7]

The 19 locks on the Dunkerton line were officially opened on 5th April, 1805. A report of that year confirms that the Radstock locks were never built, one lock, an aqueduct over Midford Brook and a tramway were sufficient owing to the lack of a regular supply from the pits served. The Coombe Hay locks soon suffered from a shortage of water. A Boulton and Watt steam pump was installed, this was guaranteed to raise 5,000 tons of water each 12 hours, enough to carry 400 tons of coal per day producing a 10% income for the Lock Fund. The pump and necessary ¾ mile extention of the upper level to the pump house cost £7,000. On 1st March, 1806 the abandoned plane, a weir and the three lower locks were purchased for £2,837 by the Fund as an insurance against accidents to the locks and pounds.[8]

Despite the raising of new £60 shares money ran out again early in 1802 and a special meeting was called at which it was hoped to raise £20,000 and a further £5,000 in Promissory notes. William Hallett, the Company Chairman, advanced £3,000, James Crowdy, chief clerk, £1,000 and William Whitworth £500.[9]

The 25th November, 1802 Company report[10] stated that inspection of the K&A and SCC had revealed that the impediments observed earlier had been removed and that, apart from the inclined plane on the latter which occasioned much delay,labour and injury by breaking the coal, there was a complete communication between the collieries and the W&B. The work of building locks in place of the plane was proceeding with vigour. "The demand for Somerset coal had now become very great on the line of the W&B and its neighbourhood. Such is the superior quality of this coal that there is no doubt that it will be carried to the east end of the canal and beyond."

The wording of the 1801 Act gave rise to problems in 1804 concerning the disposal of the income arising from the greater part of the canal then completed. The Company queried whether they were legally entitled to spend part of the tolls on maintenance or a proportion of the expenses of the Committee and their employees. A new legal adviser, Charles Durnford of Sarum, pointed out that the Act clearly and positively directed that until the canal was completed all the tolls should be divided amongst the Proprietors.[11]

Further complications arose when some Proprietors who had purchased shares at £60 or £40 believed that these, when fully paid up, were to all intents and purposes shares entitled to the same benefit and an equal division of the profits as the original £100 ones; and that the clause directing the division of profits until the canal be completed according to the sum of money actually advanced applied only to shares not fully paid up. Durnford insisted that the clause applied to all shares whether fully paid up or not. He suggested that the lower value shares were proposed as an inducement to persons to advance money and during the progress of work to receive interest thereon. When the work was completed the owners of such shares should receive equal division of the profits without any regard to the sums actually paid.

Durnford further stated that until the expiry of 10 years or until completion the Company could not redeem Promissory Notes out of the tolls and that dividends should be paid according to the positive direction of the Act "yearly and every year". No balance could be left one year to be applied in defraying any charge which might arise in the succeeding year.

Later Durnford was again asked for advice. The case is here described exactly as presented for judgement.[12]

> The W&B Company contract with Workmen to dig stone at an agreed price per yard. The stones are placed in heaps one yard in height the same in thickness and 100 yards more or less in length. When the heaps are completed they are measured by the Canal Agents and other persons are then employed at a certain price also per yard to haul them to different places upon the Canal where they are wanted to the distance of 1, 2 or 3 miles more or less. The diggers as well as the Carriers are settled with and paid monthly according to the Admeasurements by the Canal Agents of the different heaps of Stone.

It has lately been discovered that a Combination has for sometime existed between the Quarriers and the Carriers to defraud the Company.

When the piles have been completed and measured and the Carriers have taken a part of them away the Quarriers have watched their Opportunities and taken stones from the piles that were carrying away to make up fresh piles so that they have been paid twice or oftener for digging the same stone.

The Carriers too not content with that relief from their Work which the continual Depredations of the diggers afforded them have even loaded their carts from the proper piles and instead of carrying them to the places they were paid for have taken them a distance of only a few yards and shot them down by piles which were then making up so that the carriers also have been paid for hauling stone which they never removed at all or only a few yards from the spot.

These facts appear by the information of John Palmer other evidence may be obtained to corroborate his testimony.

The culprits fled upon this discovery of their conduct but they have lately returned to their Homes and bid defiance to any prosecution.

The advice given was that though morally speaking this was a fraud of great magnitude no criminal prosecution could be instituted with any prospect of success. Only strict supervision could check such practices.[13]

The 21st June, 1805 Committee report confirmed that there were then 1800 shares in the undertaking and that £65,000 would be needed to complete. At the previous meeting it had been resolved that holders of Promissory Notes would be allowed to purchase one share per note held at £25 and that each Proprietor also could buy £25 shares equal in number to his present total. This would raise £53,000. Shares created at the last meeting but not yet taken up would furnish the balance.[14]

Apparently no report was issued in 1806 for on 6th June, 1807 the Chairman reported that of the expected £53,000 only £45,570 had been raised. A meeting was called for the next month to create a sufficient number of shares to complete and at the same time suggest the propriety of making a provision for the discharge of the whole or part of the debt raised by Promissory Notes.[15]

Continuing frustration over their not being allowed to use the K&A Bath locks caused the W&B Committee on 5th December, 1806 to order Whitworth to prepare a report with a view to their seeking Counsel's advice on the legality of the ban. The report[16] outlined the earlier history; how the K&A and the Coal Canal, prior to their obtaining their first Acts, had agreed that the 6 mile common line from Limpley Stoke to Bath should be built by the K&A who would then lock down to the River Avon at Bathampton thus accommodating the whole city of Bath; how this link, so vital to the Coal Canal and later the W&B, had been promised priority; how the W&B would join the K&A and so establish a link from Bristol to their line and eventually to London and the north; how the 1798 K&A Act allowed them to extend their line to join the Avon below Pulteney Weir thus cutting off a goodly portion of Bath from canal traffic; and how, despite earlier promises, the Bath locks had not been built or communication with the Avon established by 1798.

The report described how the K&A Proprietors, held in little respect by their Committee of Management, called special meetings on 16th July that year and again on 9th February, 1800 to insist that the locks be built to establish a trade and produce a return on the money invested. A sub committee was formed which refuted the argument that there was insufficient water to operate locks, were they built. As a result work commenced and for some years boats for the K&A's convenience had used them when completed. Traders, however, were still forced to unload and convey their goods by land at great cost and inconvenience.

Whitworth reported that in 1800 the K&A had purchased a mill on the Avon near their canal 4 miles from Bath (Claverton) and made agreements with the two mills between that mill and Bath to abstract water for the canal.

By 1805 the Coal Canal was complete and the W&B well advanced, canals and Bath interests frequently applying in vain to use the locks. That year, fearing Bath and Coal Canal opposition to their seeking an Act to raise more money, the K&A signed an agreement at the House of Commons on the 31st May, not only to open the locks but also to assist Bath in promoting the building of a lock bypassing Pulteney Weir thus opening up that part of Bath earlier denied waterborne communication. They obtained their Act, but immediately forgot the agreement and the locks remained barred.

Next Spring the W&B, now becoming desperate, suggested that they would pay a fair proportion, with the other canals, of the expense of providing lockage water. John Thomas, the K&A Engineer, replied that Rennie's estimate for the machinery at Claverton was £3,000 which the K&A Committee suggested should be shared equally by themselves, the Coal Canal, the W&B and the River Avon. The W&B obviously agreed for on 26th September they wrote to the K&A to know if anything had been done in consequence of their agreement to pay their share. The Coal Canal, however, on the 29th of the same month refused to contribute stating that the K&A alone should bear the cost.

By now the W&B were convinced that the K&A were fearful of them first establishing a trade between London, Bristol and the Severn if the Bath locks were open; such a trade once established would be difficult to divert. Why else should they insist on keeping the completed locks inoperative when for the last 3 to 4 years the money paid by traders for land passage past them would have been more than sufficient to recompense the K&A for providing water either from Claverton or back pumping at Bath; besides causing traders delays and inconvenience the K&A had lost much revenue.

The 6th June, 1807 report of the W&B Chairman stated that the undertaking had suffered considerably by the K&A not supplying their locks with water at Bath to effect a communication with Bristol.

The opinion of C. Abbott of Inner Temple on 1st May, 1809 was that the Bath locks could not be used to afford a regular passage for boats without extra water supplies and although the K&A had powers for obtaining such supplies they had not done so and there was nothing in their Acts to compel them to do so. However, if at any time there was sufficient water available, then the owner of a barge probably had the right of passage upon making a proper demand and tendering the proper dues and may support an action in his own name for their refusing to open the locks. Whether or not this action would succeed was problematical.

What transpired is not certain but the Bath locks were open to all on 10th

November, 1810 and a byelaw adopted the previous July stated that until Claverton was working no barge could use the locks unless the level at the top lock stood at 5ft. The Claverton pump started work in March 1813.

The W&B suspicion that the K&A deliberately sabotaged their through traffic for as long as possible may well have been correct. As early as November 1793 John Ward, land agent to the Earl of Ailesbury and later chief clerk of the K&A, writing to the Earl, pointing out that the W&B had a great advantage over the K&A in a lower summit, much less lockage and could be executed at a much lower cost showing the necessity that the K&A should adopt the most direct and convenient line with the lowest head level and least expensive tunnel to prevent as much as possible their being rivalled by any other line. Again, in February 1795 he writes

> The W&B canal did not pretend at first to rival us in carriage, they only talked of being carriers of the internal trade of the country through which they passed but now they talk of their carrying between Bristol and London and of carrying coals to the Thames which must be in opposition to ours. I shall not be sorry if the City of London shall insist the proposed clause in the Act which will leave us in possession of the Berkshire coal trade.

The clause prohibiting the W&B coal passing beyond Reading was inserted but repealed in 1810.

The first Superintendent or Manager of the W&B was Joseph Priestley, appointed in 1810. He remained with the Company until late 1816 when he became chief clerk to the Aire and Calder Navigation, and later, in 1831, the author of the classic *Priestleys Navigable Rivers and Canals*. His salary with the W&B was £500 per annum. He purchased 13 T&S shares and invested £700 in the North Wilts. He was also on the Committee of the Severn and Wye Railway and Canal between 1814 and 1817.

In 1810 there were two grades of lock keepers, those at Chaddington, Pewsham, Calne, Melksham, Stanley, Longcot, Grove, Ardington and Abingdon being paid an average of £36 per annum. The others, probably boys, at Foxham, Dunnington and Dauntsey received only £5.4s.0d. Toll collectors were stationed at Semington, Marston, Laycock and later Latton, their salary being £54.12s.0d. Wharfingers were appointed at Abingdon, John Prince (1811, £100 p.a.), Wantage, J. Plumbe (1828, £54.12s.0d p.a.) and Marston, W. Reeve (1842, £65 p.a.). John Theobalds, the toll collector at Marston in 1810, moved to Semington in 1827 and remained there at a gradually decreasing salary until February 1867, having served the Company for 57 years.

A letter from Benjamin Moreland, a prominent Proprietor, dated 31st December, 1810 reported that he had examined the wharf book at Abingdon which showed that 100 boats had travelled up and down the canal in the first five weeks; this number would have been three times as large if the Thames had been navigable both ways. The Oxford Canal Company had a large trade at Abingdon and they were amazingly alarmed at this new opposition; a paper from their Mr Dunsford had endeavoured to rouse resistance and they were privately doing everything they could to oppose the W&B. [17]

Supplies of Somerset coal were not enough to satisfy the demand along the W&B line when it was opened throughout; William Price and Nathaniel Atherton were asked to find out why. They reported that all the pits in

Somerset from which the W&B sought supplies produced about 2,020 tons per week of which only 1,380 passed down the SCC, no supply at all coming from the Radstock line. The Semington accounts showed that the W&B imported about 516 tons per week. The real cause of the scarcity was the increased and increasing demand for coal by reason of the extension and completion of the K&A and W&B, the supply being inadequate to the demand. When they visited the Timsbury pits they found 20 boats waiting to be loaded. The country was also deprived of a considerable portion by the impediments of the SCC, navigation on this being stopped for 120 days during the last year, and at one period for two months together.[18]

W&B interests had already taken steps to overcome this shortage by seeking alternative supplies in the Forest of Dean. The coalfield there was being developed and by 1809 had two lines of communication with the Severn. The earliest was a tramway from Cinderford bridge to Bullo Pill near Newham, this being 4½ miles long with a 500 yard tunnel and later becoming part of the Forest of Dean Railway. The second line was the Severn and Wye Railway and Canal, the latter being a short link from the railhead to the river at Lydney.[19] At least three W&B Proprietors were shareholders, Ralph Gaby of Chippenham, William Whitworth and Nathaniel Atherton of Calne. The latter two also owned collieries served by the Severn and Wye.[20] How the W&B sought to tap these supplies will be seen in another chapter; any attempt to do so by using the Severn and the K&A would be uneconomic as the latter charged the highest allowable toll on all traffic to the W&B to forestall competition with their Bristol to London trade.

Despite the avowed shortage of Somerset coal and lack of communication with their interests in the Forest of Dean the W&B petitioned Parliament early in 1810 for powers to repeal the clause in the 1795 Act forbidding the carriage of W&B borne coal below Reading. Despite objections from coal interests in the North East the Bill was passed as *50 Geo. 111 Cap. 148.* The clause was repealed, a new limit of the City Stone at Staines was imposed, this being where the jurisdiction of the Thames Commissioners ended and that of the City of London began. There is no record of the Company ever taking advantage of this Act; it was, probably, obtained in hopes of a large traffic in Forest coal when the 1810 proposals matured.

Before the Annual General Meeting of 6th April, 1811 rumours were circulating that all was not well with the W&B and the fact that navigation was impossible for some months seemed to lend weight to these. Both the Chairman and Whitworth felt it necessary to boost morale by suitable explanations. The Chairman's report held veiled doubts about the financial prospects of the Company.

> At the present juncture, many circumstances not at all concerned with the future prospects of the Concern, combine to depreciate the price of all property which has not had its value ascertained by a matured income; but the Committee have no reason whatsoever to abate in the expectation they have heretofore formed of the ultimate advantages of the undertaking.

Whitworth's excuse for the prolonged shutdown admitted that some of the constructional work on locks had not been up to standard,

> The communication between London and Bath being prevented during the last summer by repairs to the K&A, I considered that the least inconvenience would arise to the Traders by making the necessary repairs to the W&B at the same time.

The heads of many of the locks were taken down and repaired, the canal in many places cleaned out, and the whole could not be completed till the latter part of October.

He denied rumours that water supplies were inadequate; Wroughton and Wanborough Brooks which supplied the summit level could supply 47 locks per day in the driest season, and for at least seven months of the year this could be increased to 100. On either side of the summit many additional supplies could be taken, for example from the River Marden at Calne and Beckett Brook at Shrivenham.[21]

On 25th July, 1812 the Committee resolved to pay a dividend of seven shillings per share on the 7,436 effective shares[22]; they later decided not to pay any more until all the works had been completed and all debts paid off.

Early in 1813 the Bishop of Durham petitioned Parliament that nothing in the 1795 Act empowered the Company to alter, divert or make any use of springs through the estates of Samuel Barrington and the Petitioner in the Tything of Beckett in the Parish of Shrivenham. The clauses in the Act had proved ineffectual, the estates were suffering injury, no agreement could be reached with the Company so permission was sought to introduce a Bill for protecting the estates. The W&B petitioned against the Bill but no counsel appeared on their behalf until after the second reading. Then Mr Estcourt appeared, not to oppose but to clear the name of James Crowdy who was in the unfortunate position of being both the Clerk for the Company and Steward of the Beckett Property. Estcourt pointed out that the original clause had been drawn up with the full knowledge of the Bishop and some additional words inserted in his handwriting. The Act, 53 Geo. 111 Cap. 120 received the Royal Assent on 3rd June, 1813. Water could only be taken from Idston Brook; the Company were to fill in a cut taking water from a stream running from Ashbury to Idston Brook. To supply water to a farm a pipe of 1 inch diameter was to be laid through the dam or dams confining the water of the Brook.[23]

Tolls rose steadily over the years but Priestley thought they could be improved. In September 1813 he wrote to the Committee asking to be allowed to charge the full Parliamentary toll on corn to places along the canal where no other conveyance could interfere. He admitted that tolls on through trade must be reduced to compete with the K&A but why should Swindon, Wootton Bassett, Calne and Chippenham benefit? The full toll from Wantage to Chippenham, a distance of 39 miles, would be six shillings and sixpence per ton instead of the four shillings charged. He suggested that this should be increased to four shillings and sixpence at first to see what the reaction of Traders would be. The result of this and similiar suggested squeezes is not known.

The financial worries of the Company were by no means over; on 24th November, 1814 they petitioned Parliament that they would not be able to complete the works unless they were able to raise more money as the sum subscribed under the first and second Acts was insufficient. The resulting Act, 55 Geo. 111 Cap. 4 empowered them to raise another £100,000 or as much as might be necessary by shares or Promissory Notes, to buy their own shares, to subscribe up to £15,000 to the North Wilts and to form a sinking fund. Further shares were issued at £25 and finally at £12.10s.0d.

References

1   CL 12 & 13 Chippenham Borough records.
2   CL 15, BRO D EEL 07 bundle 1
3   K.R. Clew, The Somersetshire Coal Canal.
4   CL 17.
5   CL 18.
6   CL 20.
7   Priestley. Navigable Rivers and Canals.
8   WRO 212A/27/21/3.
9   SRLG 1002.
10 SRLG 1004 CL 22.
11 CL 25.
12 CL 26 & 27.
13 CL 28.
14 CL 29.
15 CL 30.
16 CL 31.
17 SRLG.
18 SRLG 1007.
19 Priestley.
20 WRO 212A/27/21/3.
21 SRLG 1002.
22 TS 207 20/8.
23 JHC Vol 60 p207.
TS Thames and Severn papers, Gloucester Record Office.
JHC Journal of the House of Commons.

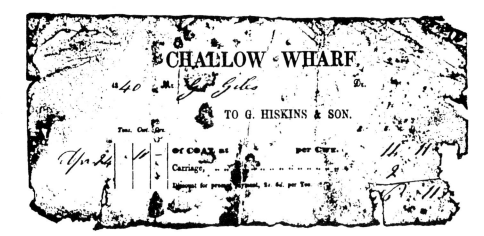

Chapter Five

Plans for Expansion 1810

Before the W&B was completed, and while the Company was heavily in debt, notices of three costly proposals were published within a period of four months. These concerned the linking of the canal with the Grand Junction at Marsworth, with the Severn via Bristol and with the Thames and Severn summit level.

The first, dated 23rd March, 1810 was circulated to all Proprietors and stated that the W&B intended to apply to Parliament in the next session for powers to build a canal from Abingdon to Marsworth, a distance of 36½ miles to join the W&B and the GJ, the link to be known as "The Western Junction Canal". The estimated cost was £220,000.[1] This line had already been sur-veyed by William Whitworth as noted in the previous chapter.

The second notice, dated 12th April, 1810, was entitled "Proposed Canal from Bristol to the Wilts and Berks". A meeting was to be held at the Angel Inn Chippenham on 5th May to consider making a canal from the City of Bristol to the W&B at or near Foxham, passing through the Gloucestershire coalfield near Coalpit Heath and Pucklechurch. Whitworth had surveyed the 29½ mile line and reported that lime and stone were plentiful along the course; this would make the construction of locks and other works more easy. By use of this canal, the W&B and the earlier proposed Western Junction an uninterrupted canal line would be provided between Bristol and London 154 miles long, not only shorter than any other so far proposed but also "entirely free from the delays and difficulties inseparable from River navigation, and by the connection with the Grand Junction there would also be opened a canal route to the North of England."

The alternative route from Bristol to London consisted of 93 miles of the Avon and K&A and 78 miles of the Thames below Reading, a total of 171 miles. The Company claimed, rather optimistically, that their transit time throughout would be 3 to 4 days and the toll thirty-six shillings to thirty-seven shillings per ton. They stated that apart from the obvious benefit such a speedy and certain communication with London would bring to the inhabi-tants of Bristol, they would also obtain cheaper coal from the Gloucester pits, the alternative method of carriage being over roads "continually broken up by the passage of heavy wagons." The whole of the country traversed by the projected line would also be supplied from this source and the W&B would be provided with an alternative supply to Somerset coal; the competition would be beneficial to consumers. The iron, copper and tin works of South Wales would also benefit by the proposed route which would carry their goods to London at a small expense "without the delays to which they are now subject."[1]

We will see later that this Bristol Junction proposal was abandoned on the insistence of the T&S in return for their support for the third scheme. This was dated 22nd June, 1810 and stated that Whitworth had surveyed the country between the W&B and T&S and found that a junction might be formed by a canal from Wootton Bassett on the former to Ewen on the summit level of the latter. He stated that such a line would be easy to build and well supplied with water, but if it were built the T&S would have to alter their locks between their summit and Brimscombe Port; for this rather drastic suggestion he offered no reason.

The W & B Company resolved that all the necessary proceedings preparatory to an application to Parliament in the next session should be taken; Messrs Crowdy and Whitworth were ordered to draw up plans and books of reference. The undertaking was to be called "The Severn Junction Canal". Crowdy was directed to approach the T & S to ascertain whether they would modify their locks and at the same time inform them that any water taken would be pumped back though there was a strong possibility that a substantial supply would be provided to them.[1] If such plans etc. were prepared they have not been found.

In all these proposals the Company painted the rosiest of pictures neglecting to point out that they were for narrow canals with probably 144 locks between Bristol and London which would put them at a disadvantage as far as through trade was concerned.

At this time other schemes were on foot to bypass the lower Thames. The K & A were considering a link between their line near Newbury to the head of the Basingstoke Canal to be known as "The Hants and Berks Junction Canal". Rennie had surveyed the "Western Union" between Maidenhead and Uxbridge and also two bypasses, one from Reading to Windsor and the second from Datchet to Isleworth.

These schemes naturally aroused the ire of the Thames Commisioners; at their meeting at Oxford on 29th December, 1810 two reports were produced "On the objectives and consequences of several projected canals which interfere with the interests of the River Thames." One, by John Hore of the Kennet Navigation does not concern this story; the second by Edward Lovenden Lovenden is a wonderful example of perverted argument inspired by fear of personal financial loss. We will see in the chapter on the North Wilts why he was so antagonistic to any proposal which threatened the navigation of the Upper Thames, and how the Severn Junction proposal was modified to a link between Latton on the T & S and Swindon on the W & B. Lovenden's report stated that "from Latton is to be derived that supply of water for which it is well known that both the W & B and the GJ stand much in need". He claimed that the W & B were to pump back the water taken from their summit by the canal to Latton and further accused the T & S of pumping Ewen Springs at Thames Head, this water then to be pumped up to the W & B summit and allowed to flow east to the GJ. He was rather naive when he expected water to flow 186 ft uphill from the W & B. He also accused the W & B of urging on a canal from Stratford on Avon to Witney and planning to unite with that line by an aqueduct at or near Newbridge for which purpose water would also have to be supplied from the Thames. He declared that no agreement had been concluded between the W & B and T & S and stated that, in his opinion, the whole London trade would use the Marsworth link should it be built. The one solid piece of evidence he produced was a quotation from Robert Whitworth's 1793 report to the W & B subscribers, "There is little or no obstruction on the Thames below Abingdon, stoppages for the last year did not total more than a fortnight's delay."[2]

The Lovenden objections were refuted in a Public notice issued on 13th March by the W & B Chairman which stated that the Severn Junction would

be forbidden by its Bill to take water from Thames springs and that the
Company had never urged on the canal proposed to be made to Stratford nor
had they ever had any interview or communication with its promoters.
Lovenden himself had poured scorn on the upper Thames as impossible for
navigation when in 1785 he had supported the proposed canal from Lechlade
to Abingdon.

> Not only had the T&S agreed to the SJ but they had also petitioned Parliament in its
> favour. Having expended upwards of £300,000, they find the wretched navigation
> of the river from Lechlade to Oxford such a bar to their success that they are now
> willing to sacrifice the tolls on the Latton to Inglesham part of their canal concluding
> that the increase in trade on the remainder will amply repay them. The SJ would
> greatly increase the trade below Abingdon which would compensate the Thames
> Commissioners for that lost above and any injury to Mr Lovenden's lock at Buscot
> and other private locks might be the subject of compensation before a Committee of
> the House of Commons.

To this notice Whitworth added a report that the W&B were empowered to
take 7,131 tons of water per day even in the driest season, enough for 47
locks. For seven months of the year this would be increased to 100. The
proposed Coate reservoir would cover 50 acres and contain 4,125 locks, this,
together with the 480 which could be drawn from the summit, would provide
enough water for 77 locks per day during the five driest months. Thus
supplies were ample for both the W&B and the SJ even if the water for the
latter were not pumped back.[3]

The Gloucestershire Record Office has preserved a large plan of the
Stratford project Lovenden referred to and another of a canal from Wootton
Bassett on the W&B to join one belonging to the Bristol Dock Company. Both
plans are obviously the work of the same person, the former is inscribed
"Surveyed by F Bartley 1810".[4] This canal, to be known as the Central
Junction is shown leaving the W&B at Abingdon, following the River
Windrush as far as Longborough and passing through Burford, Bourton on
the Water and Shipton on Stour with a branch to Naunton. It was surveyed
under the supervision of John Rennie whose estimate for the 60 miles was
£470,000. Opposition from the GJ and Oxford canals was violent and the
project never reached Parliament.

The second of these lines was to leave the W&B at Vastern Wharf passing
Brinkworth, Malmesbury, Pucklechurch and Mangotsfield with a tunnel at
West Littleton.[4] Little more is known of the lines or their promoters but in
November 1810 the T&S Committee resolved to oppose the Central Junction,
a canal from Tewkesbury to Woodstock near Oxford and that from the W&B
to Malmesbury and Bristol.[5]

The Western Junction proposal did not die so easily. Although initially the
W&B supported the scheme they lost interest then the GJ imposed conditions unacceptable to them. They, the GJ, to protect their lucrative trade in
coal and iron from the Midlands, demanded a compensation of two shillings
and sixpence for every ton of coal passing beyond Thame and four shillings
for every ton of iron from Wales the moment it entered their canal.[6] At this
time too the K&A were planning a 12 mile link between Maidenhead and
Cowley on the GJ this being surveyed by Rennie. No doubt the latter required

similiar compensations from the K&A; this proposed line also died a lingering death.

Early in 1811 Aylesbury interests introduced a Bill for a canal from the GJ Aylesbury branch to Sutton Wick near Abingdon. £1,698 was paid to engineers and surveyors, £1,943 to solicitors and £132 to a Parliamentary agent. The Bill did not survive its first reading.[7]

On 16th August, 1817 a meeting between the W&B and Western Junction Committees was announced, at this it was agreed that the junction and line be reconsidered.[8] In the same year an anonymous broadsheet was published extolling the virtues of the link; it included a comprehensive map of all the connecting canals.

On August 1819 Thomas Telford produced yet another survey at the joint expense of the W&B and GJ. From Abingdon basin his line ran south, parallel to the river. One lock was needed to gain sufficient height to be able to cross the Thames on a cast iron aqueduct 6ft above the highest flood level. This line then followed closely that surveyed by Whitworth in 1803. The estimate was for £198,725.19s.0d.

On 14th January, 1828 Robert Hedges of Thame, midway between Aylesbury and Abingdon, wrote to the Editor of the *Oxford Journal* complained that nothing had been done and stating that he had in his office some 400 plans for the Western Junction. The GJ branch to Aylesbury was complete and working so there were 6 miles less to cut; this branch had bought the most expensive land and constructed 16 locks from Marsworth. He drew a harrowing picture of the good people of Thame paying an exorbitant price for their coal and pleaded with the W&B to foster the connection and so improve their line. He also wrote to the W&B Manager, William Dunsford asking for particulars of the Company's trade and their views of the proposed line. Dunsford's reply on 5th August, 1828 confirms why the W&B were not interested.

> You are doubtless aware that the Grand Junction Company as the price of their consent to allow the communication at Aylesbury demand a compensation for coal and iron passing into their canal – should such a tax on the trade be conceded it would be entirely subversive to the idea of profits to the Proprietors from these articles. But Lord Shaftesbury sets his face against compensation clauses between Companies at all, and although his Lordship is not invincible, he is at all times a most formidable adversary. The Oxford Canal Company and Old Father Thames you of course have made up your mind to fight, they are adversaries with whom there can be no compromise.[9]

Lord Shaftesbury was Chairman of the House of Lords Committee dealing with canal bills.

Despite this dampening advice Hedges published a pamphlet announcing a meeting at Thame on 28th August, the Earl of Macclesfield taking the Chair. A Committee was formed and a fund of £200,000 set up. An Engineer was to be appointed to make plans and an estimate; he was also to consider whether a railway would be preferable to a canal.[10]

On 4th November W.A. Provis, the chosen Engineer and a pupil of Telford, produced his plan, again similiar to Whitworths, and an estimate of £171,717.0s.3d for a line 27¾ miles long falling 87ft from Aylesbury by 13

CANAL TO THAME.

Sketch, shewing at one view the situation of the Canals
which would be connected by the proposed Cut.

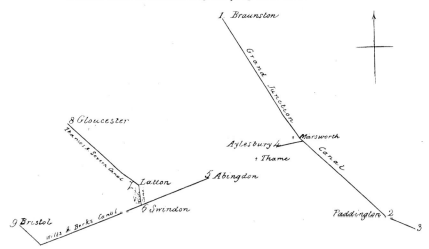

1 *Braunston*. At this Village the Grand Junction unites with the Oxford
and Coventry Canal, which passes on Northward, joining other Canals, making
a complete Inland Navigation to Liverpool; by which conveyance Government
send troops and Stores, by water; from London to Ireland.

1. Grand Junction Canal to
2. Paddington.
3. Extent of Regent Canal at the Docks below London Bridge.
4. Aylesbury, from which is the proposed Canal by Thame to
5. Abingdon.
6. Swindon.
7. Latton to
8. Gloucester is by the Thames & Severn, & Berkley & Gloucester Canals.
   From Swindon 6 is by the Wilts & Berks Canal to
9. Bristol.

If the short distance were made navigable by the proposed Canal from
4 to 5, a complete water conveyance for the produce of the Manufacturing
District in the Counties of Leicester, Nottingham, Lancaster, York, &c. would
be obtained by the Inland Counties through which the line of Navigation
would pass. A Meeting to take the same into consideration, will be held
at the Town Hall, Thame, on Thursday 28th of August inst: at One Oclock.
The Earl of Macclesfield will take the Chair.

Rob.t Hedges

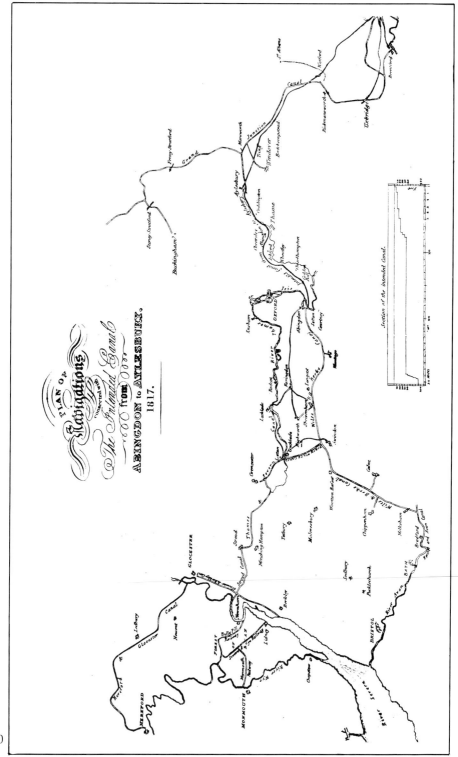

PLAN OF
Navigations
connected with
The Intended Canal
from
ABINGDON to AYLESBURY.
1817.

Section of the intended Canal.

Intended Extension of the Wilts and Berks Canal.

THE different Lines of Inland Navigation between the Ports of Bristol and London, from their connexion with the Thames, and consequent exposure to the numerous obstructions and difficulties attendant on the passage of that River, have hitherto failed of becoming a regular and expeditious channel of conveyance between those important Cities; and through a vast expence, has been incurred in making the Canals, and improving the navigation of the River, a very large portion of the Trade is still carried on by means of Wagons.

The proposed Extension of the Wilts and Berks Canal to join a collateral branch of the Grand Junction at Aylesbury, a cut of only thirty miles in length, would at once establish a perfect Canal communication between Bath and the Metropolis, whereby the various commodities brought from Bristol by the Avon might be conveyed throughout in the short space of four days, at one third of the expence of land carriage, and without the inconvenience of transhipping.

By means of the North Wilts Canal (now in train for a speedy completion) a direct communication would also be opened between the River Severn and London, through the Stroud and Thames and Severn Canals, which will be also independent of any intermediate river navigation. By this channel large quantities of the heavy products of the Mining Districts of South Wales, and of Stone, Timber, and Coal from the Forest of Dean, may be confidently expected to pass; and the City of Gloucester, and the populous manufacturing and agricultural county surrounding it, would obtain an efficient water conveyance for the interchange of its various products and commodities with the Metropolis now carried by land, or by very circuitous routes.

The intended continuation of the Gloucester and Berkely Canal to join the Stroud will also give additional importance to the proposed new cut.

A slight inspection of the above PLAN will at once shew the great and obvious advantages of the scheme in a commercial point of view, as its execution will give the utmost possible facility to the trading intercourse between the Port of London, and the Counties of Berks, Wilts, Somerset, Glocester, Hereford, and Monmouth, the Cities of Bristol, Bath, and Gloucester, and all parts of South Wales.

The distances will be as follows :

	Miles
From Bristol to Bath, by the Avon	17
Bath to Semington, by the Kennet and Avon	15
Semington to Abingdon, by the Wilts and Berks	59
Abingdon to Aylesbury, by the proposed Canal	30
Aylesbury to London, by the Grand Junction	54

151 Miles of Canal.

From the Severn :	Miles
The Stroud Canal	8
Thames and Severn ditto	20
North Wilts ditto	8¼
Wilts and Berks ditto	25¼
Intended Canal	30
Aylesbury to London, per Grand Junction	54
Total	**146**

Canal from Aylesbury by Thame to Abingdon.

At a Meeting held at the Town Hall, Thame, on Thursday the 28th day of August, 1828, pursuant to Notice, to take into consideration the propriety of applying to Parliament for a Bill for making a navigable Canal from Aylesbury, by Thame, to join the Wilts and Berks Canal at Abingdon.

The EARL of MACCLESFIELD, *Chairman.*

It was resolved—

1. That a Canal from the Branch of the Grand Junction Canal, at or near Aylesbury, by way of the Town of Thame, to communicate with the Wilts and Berks Canal, at or near Abingdon, will be of great public utility, by opening a direct and complete communication between the Western part of the Kingdom and the Metropolis, and connecting the whole of the Inland Navigations of the Kingdom, and will also be of local advantage to the Country through which the Line of such Canal will be carried.

2. Several Plans having been proposed.—Resolved, that a Committee be appointed to employ a Surveyor and Engineer to examine minutely the several Lines and make Plans and Sections of such of them as shall appear to the Committee most proper, and to ascertain with accuracy the names of the Parishes, Hamlets and Proprietors of Lands through which the Canal will pass, together with the means of supplying the same with Water and effecting a Junction with the Canals abovementioned, and to make an Estimate of the Costs and other necessary Expences attending the same, and also to consider of the propriety of forming the proposed communication by a Rail Road instead of a Canal, and report the same to a General Meeting to be convened by the Committee.

3. That such Committee consist of—

The Earl of Macclesfield,	John Blackall, Esq.
Sir Scrope B. Morland, Bart.	John Brown, Esq.
John Fane, Esq. M. P.	The Rev. C. L. Kerby,
P. T. Wykeham, Esq.	The Rev. C. F. Spencer,
C. C. Dormer, Esq.	Mr. Harry Lupton,
Dr. John Lee,	Mr. Robert Hedges,

4. That a Fund of £200,000 be raised by Shares of £25 each, and a Deposit of Ten Shillings per Share be paid at the time of subscribing, and that Books be opened at the following Bankers for the receipt of Deposits, viz. Messrs. Morland and Co. and Messrs. Praeds and Co. *London*; Messrs. Rickford and Son, *Aylesbury*; Messrs. Walker and Co. Messrs. Parsons and Co. Messrs. Cox and Co. Messrs. Wotton and Co. *Oxford*; Messrs. Knapp, *Abingdon*; Messrs. Cozens, *Wallington*; Mr. Thomas Stone and Mr. John Page, *Thame.*

5. That the thanks of the Meeting be given to the Right Honorable the Earl of Macclesfield for the handsome manner in which he has offered to promote the object of this Meeting, and for his attendance and impartial conduct in the Chair.

6. That the thanks of the Meeting be also given to Mr. Robert Hedges for the trouble he has taken in bringing the measure forward, and assembling the present Meeting.

H. Bradford, Printer, Thame.

locks. But all in vain, subscriptions were not forthcoming and the GJ would not relax the compensation claim. The last mention of the Western Junction comes in a letter from Dunsford to Palmer of Thame on 30th January, 1829, "As from the state of the subscriptions and the negotiations with the Grand Junction Company, I apprehend that you will not be able to go to Parliament in the ensuing Sessions."[9]

References

1   TS 207/20/1, 2 & 3.
2   Swindon Goddard papers 1021.
3   Gloucester City Library JX14.25.
4   TS 175/17.
5   TS 164C.
6   TS 207/15.
7   JHC Vol 66 p76.
8   TS 207/17.
9   Swindon, letter book.
10 BRO DEL/07.

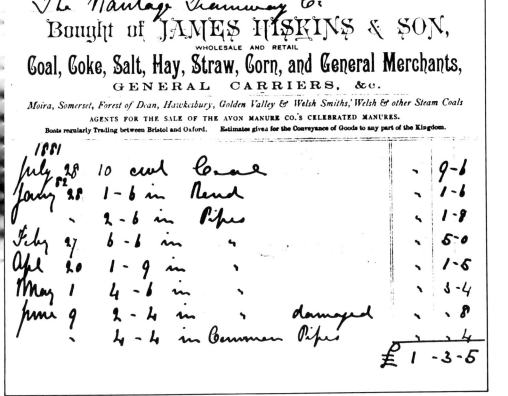

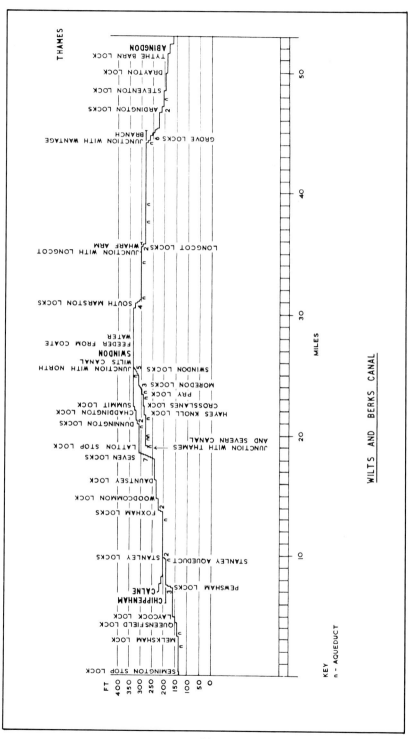

An elevation plan of system.

WILTS AND BERKS CANAL

Chapter Six
The North Wilts 1810–1820

Of the three 1810 schemes it is obvious that the one which would best serve the W&B and be the least costly to build was the Severn Junction. They required an alternative supply of coal having experienced difficulty in obtaining a sufficiently large quantity from the SCC and had, as we have seen, made some preparations for procuring this from the Forest of Dean. There were two possible routes from the Forest to the W&B. The Bristol Junction would open the way to the Severn without the expensive aid of the K&A; the Severn Junction, however, would be only half the length, an easier line to build and would make use of the T&S already deeply involved in the Forest coal trade.

The T&S would obviously support the Severn Junction proposal in preference to the Bristol Junction which would threaten their trade with South Wales, and by providing another line for the distribution of South Wales and Forest coal would deprive them of the tolls they would collect from this trade and the coal supplied to the W&B via the Severn Junction.

The estimated cost of the Bristol Junction is not known, but it would have been a difficult and expensive line to build, involving some 70 locks. By tapping the Gloucestershire coalfield it would provide a further alternative supply of coal both for Bristol and the W&B but as far as is known the W&B Proprietors had no such financial interest in this field as they had in the Forest of Dean. There had been talk in 1803 of the W&B obtaining coal from these pits by means of a railway from Pucklechurch to the River Avon. The K&A were prepared to support any such proposal but nothing was done at this time; the railway was built in 1832, the K&A being the majority shareholders.[1]

The W&B lost interest in the Bristol Junction when the GJ claimed heavy compensation for all coal and iron imported into their canal from an extended W&B; the W&Bs grandiose scheme of an all canal line from Bristol to London became much less attractive.

The T&S had another good reason for preferring the Severn Junction; it offered them a chance of bypassing the poor upper Thames navigation which had always been unsatisfactory to their interests. Since their canal had opened in 1789 the Company had been fighting a running battle with the Thames Commissioners trying to induce them to improve the river. An Act of 1795 had empowered the Commissioners to carry out improvements to the navigation; money had been subscribed for the purpose but despite the building of a number of locks above Oxford little real improvement had materialised. In 1797 James Black in a report to the T&S Committee suggested that a road be built between their canal at Inglesham and Acorn Bridge on the line of the W&B,

> . . . so that by a land carriage of 7 miles from canal to canal Abingdon etc may be supplied with coals and in bad water times goods by the same carriage may be forwarded to Abingdon and avoid the river. Such are the benefits that will accrue from the making of this road and ultimately prove the advantage of a communication by a 7 mile canal by the vale of the Acorn Brook (now the River Cole) to the W&B canal.[2]

No action was taken.

In the 1810 proposal Whitworth stated that if the Severn Junction was built the T&S would have to alter their locks between their summit and Brimscombe Port. This suggestion would only be valid if the T&S renounced boats wider and longer than the narrow boats capable of navigating the W&B. Presumably he was concerned about the waste of water involved in the passage of smaller boats through locks 92 ft long and 13 ft wide. The 68 ft locks below Brimscombe could by careful manoeuvring accommodate 72 ft boats diagonally across the 16 ft wide chamber.

A meeting between representatives of the two Companies was held at Abingdon on 14th July, 1810. The W&B agreed to forget the Bristol Junction and build the Severn Junction but not on the lines earlier suggested by Whitworth and Black. The W&B end of the link was to be at or near Swindon and the T&S end at or near Cricklade below Latton lock. It was resolved that "The union of the two canals will be of very great Public Utility and of advantage to the Proprietors of both Concerns, allowing the T&S to bypass the bad upper Thames navigation."[3] This agreement was a compromise, James Black again proposed his line between Shrivenham and Inglesham; this would be shorter and allow the T&S to use the whole length of their canal, but would increase tolls on coal to the W&B and introduce it some way east of the centre of the line. The Earl of Peterborough again turned this proposal down stating that while he personally favoured the idea he feared that Lord Radnor and Mr Warnford would bring unsurmountable difficulties on account of their extensive water meadows at Shrivenham.

Black also urged the T&S to support the W&B in promoting the Abingdon–Marsworth link which would bypass the lower Thames; he argued that the double threat might stimulate the Thames Commissioners into action. Subsequent to the meeting he proposed that a regulating lock should be built with a one foot fall from the Severn Junction to the T&S; this he stated would ensure amiable relations between the two Companies considering that the loss of water incurred by the Severn Junction by the inclusion of such a lock would be slight compared with the sacrifice the T&S would bear in allowing 20 ton boats to use their locks capable of passing 60 tons.

Whitworth too had second thoughts; he was concerned about the danger of floods damaging both canals. The agreed site of the junction meant that at the crossing of the Thames the Severn Junction level would be only 2 ft above the Thames surface. He proposed altering the site to Redfurlong Bridge ¾ mile above Latton lock thus bringing the SJ level 9½ ft above the river.[4] This proposal was accepted and the flood danger also minimised by carrying the canal over arches allowing flood water to pass underneath. The regulating lock, however, was not built until 1826 and then only after the very unfriendly relationship Black had sought to avoid.

News of the agreement aroused strong opposition particularly from Thames interests. Lord Redesdale of Batsford wrote to the W&B claiming that his 40 years experience of canal Acts had proved "a greater sum of injustice and opression had never been produced by any legislative measure in any country." He could see no possible advantages which his property or those nearby could derive from the SJ, indeed he saw great injury. "I know that canals produce great evils even when they are most advantageous, and that those evils are greatly increased by the officious manner in which the powers given to the adventurers are exercised."[5]

The belief that the SJ would take water from the Thames had not yet been effectively scotched; rumours began to circulate which the W&B denied in a notice of 27th November, 1810, "Observations as to the intended Severn Junction Canal." In this Whitworth asserted that the canal had no intention of taking any water from the Thames over and above the 3,700 tons per day already supplied to the W&B by the Wanborough feeder, this quantity being sufficient for 24 locks. The W&B were empowered to build a reservoir at Coate and had also purchased land at Trow Lane, Tockenham for another to supply the lower levels west of Swindon. Apart from these large reserves, the summit level had been excavated 2 ft deeper and 6 ft wider than elsewhere, this extra stock of water could supply 10 locks per day for one month. There was therefore absolutely no need for water to be taken from the Thames at Cricklade.[5] Having thus attempted to reassure the Thames interests he proceeded to make a suggestion which he must have known would be highly unpopular with the T&S. He proposed that the SJ should be on a level for the 3½ miles between the T&S and the intended locks at Widdel Hill, that the supply for these locks be pumped from the SJ by an engine and then discharged back to the SJ, and that a regulating lock be built at the junction with the W&B.[5] The T&S would not countenance this suggestion that they should supply all necessary water. The finished canal had no such engine or regulating lock. The final 3½ miles was level and only stop gates protected T&S water.

A Bill for the SJ was introduced in the House of Commons on 12th February, 1811 and immediately the University of Oxford lodged a petition against it. To this the W&B retaliated with a broadsheet in which Mr Hallett expressed "great astonishment at finding the University of Oxford petitioning against a canal which would so much benefit the poor of their City by producing a competition in coal as well as increasing the Tolls collected at their own lock called Boulters."[6] This lock near Maidenhead would benefit from the extra trade resulting from the building of the SJ.

The Bill was given its first reading on 4th March and during the following two weeks a veritable flood of objections poured in, mainly from towns along the Thames who feared that the money they had subscribed to the Commissioners would be in jeopardy. The Oxford Canal Company joined the petitioners against; they faced increased competition in their large coal trade which had hitherto been partly protected from the invasion of Forest coal by the difficulties on the upper Thames. The T&S naturally petitioned in favour stating "the navigation of the Thames was imperfect, precarious and dangerous and because of it the expectations of this Company had fallen very short."[2] The Bill was then hastily withdrawn as it was suddenly realised that the T&S would also have to apply for a Bill to make the junction with their canal.[13]

Whitworth, who had been appointed as Engineer for the project, produced his estimate for the SJ in July 1811; if the Swindon termination were to be at

Eastcott his figure was £60,000 and if at Swindon Wharf, £62,000. The fall of 59 feet from Swindon to Latton was to be divided into 11 locks to conserve water and the estimated price had been reduced by planning to cut for nearly 3 miles besides roads and across common land.[5] He weakened his previous argument that W & B water supplies were ample by this admission that there was a need to conserve water and also by asking that the Bill should seek to raise up to £10,000 for the building of Coate reservoir.

Violent opposition to any scheme for bypassing the upper Thames could always be expected from Edward Loveden Loveden, sometime M.P. for Abingdon, a prominent Thames Commissioner and a Proprietor of both the T & S and W & B. This opposition is easy to understand; Loveden owned Buscot lock near Lechlade. Not only was his toll of one shilling for every five tons passing as high as any on the Thames but he also charged another similar toll for the return journey, this double toll being unique on the river. This charge was in operation from as early as 1771 to 1821. The tolls collected for March 1791 were £8.10s.0d representing the passage of some 400 tons.[7] This is a surprisingly small figure and an indication of the restriction of trade imposed on the T & S by the state of the upper Thames, at this date their line being open for 18 months.[8]

Loveden called a special General Meeting of the T & S Proprietors at the Globe Tavern, London on 7th January, 1812. Whitworth and Atherton, whose interest in the Forest of Dean we have already noted, attended; they were both T & S Proprietors, Whitworth holding 18 shares and Atherton 14. It was resolved

> that it is in the interest of the T & S to cooperate with the Thames Commissioners in making every practical improvement in the navigation from Lechlade to London, that from observations of very expensive works recently judiciously made at Culham, from information of others equally important actually ordered at Clifton and of more intended to be made with all possible despatch, and from reliance on the further assurances given by the Commissioners that the whole river within their jurisdiction should be forthwith be made an effectual navigation, the Proprietors of the T & S do not at present perceive any necessity for a junction with the W & B at Latton and therefore judge it now not expedient to consent thereto.

The resolution was passed by 572 share votes to 401.[7]

This complete about face provoked John Disney, the T & S Chairman, into writing a long letter, dated 18th February, 1812, addressed to all the T & S Proprietors and pointing out the dangers involved. He outlined the history of the SJ project and described how the W & B committee had been persuaded to drop the Bristol Junction in favour of the SJ; how the 1811 application for an Act had to be abandoned as the T & S could not prepare their application in time, but that early in January 1812 both parties were ready to reapply to Parliament as they had agreed to the junction. At the meeting on 7th January a certain Thames Commissioner had attended and stated that a Bill was about to be presented to Parliament for the improvement of that river between Abingdon and the T & S and because of this statement a resolution was passed that the T & S should withdraw their consent. At this meeting there were, apart from himself, only two Proprietors who were acting members of the Committee, and they did not vote on the question at all. It was supported by some gentlemen who had come to town for that purpose, but whom he had not seen more than once before at any meeting over the past twelve years. He had since searched the register of the Private Bill office and no petition for any such Bill could be found. The sudden reversal of policy had so disgusted the SJ promoters that they had given up their project. The W & B, wishing to improve their canal, and having large properties in the Forest of Dean in stone and coal mines, finding that they could not reach them with the aid of the T & S sought the communication otherwise. They projected a line from Foxham to Berkeley, "a measure pregnant with the most destructive consequences to us and calling for opposition to the last shilling of our resources." Certain members representing 747 shares had met on 14th February 14th to discuss what should be done; they decided to call a General meeting to reconsider the January resolution. The facts he would lay before the meeting would convince them that unless the resolution was revoked their Company would perhaps be totally destroyed. He urged all Proprietors to attend.[9]

This meeting was held on 18th March. Disney pointed out that the works noted in the January resolution were of remote interest only to the T & S and that a conference with the Commissioners had disclosed that no new works were ordered or contemplated. It was resolved that the junction would be highly beneficial and that all necessary steps should be taken to revive and promote the SJ. It was also resolved that application should be made to the Commissioners to pay out a specific sum of the money they had collected to improve the Lechlade–Oxford section.[8] Two years later the Commissioners were to admit to the W & B that it was wholly out of their power to do so.[10]

Deputations from the two Companies met at the Castle Inn, Marlborough on 18th July, 1812, the chair being taken by Lord Radnor representing the W & B. Some of the details on which both would consent to the junction were settled, of these the most important concerning Forest coal. This was to be entitled to such discounts as would reduce the toll taken by the T & S to two shillings and sixpence per ton, and as an added inducement to its importation to the W & B, boats returning empty having delivered such coal would be exempted from all tolls. No such concession was to apply to Somerset coal entering the T & S although each Company agreed to compensate the other for all foreign coal imported. The W & B were to supply all water for the SJ and not pump any back. Finally a recommendation was made that a general meeting of each Company should agree to provide one third of the cost leaving one third to be subscribed by landowners and the general public.[11] This was not a popular suggestion at a later meeting of the T & S Proprietors despite the great advantages they expected from the canal; the truth was that they did not have £20,000 on hand nor could they hope to raise such a sum.[2] The W & B did not improve their predicament by issuing a notice stating that although the proposed canal promised a fair return on its cost, as the principal beneficiaries would be the two canal Companies, the public could hardly be expected to raise the sum alloted to them. The potential of the project was demonstrated by the fact that the value of W & B shares rose when the SJ was agreed, and fell again when it appeared that the T & S had withdrawn their consent.[12]

The next joint meeting was held at the Ram Inn, Cirencester on 14th August with John Disney in the chair. He reported later that the meeting was well attended, many people being there who had no financial interest in

TO THE PROPRIETORS

THAMES AND SEVERN CANAL.

GENTLEMEN,

As an individual proprietor in the Thames and Severn Canal, whose stake in that concern, together with others of my family, is something considerable, amounting to no less a sum, on the original value of shares, than £33,900 (above one eighth of the whole) I feel excused in addressing myself, on the present state of our affairs, to you who are mutually interested in the same cause.

I am particularly anxious to lay before you, a full and candid statement of our very critical situation at this time, owing to several circumstances of great importance, which have taken place in our concern within the last three or four years. In thus addressing the proprietors with a view to put them in possession of facts, which it is important they should be acquainted with, before the day of our next general assembly, I beg to be considered as acting only as an individual, and without involving in the merit or demerit of the measure I am taking, those gentlemen with whom I have so long and so cordially acted ; whose aim, as well as my own, has uniformly been the ultimate good and permanent improvement of the Thames and Severn Canal in all its relations whether internal or external.

I shall forthwith, therefore, proceed to relate, as shortly as possible those things which altogether, en masse, will form the subject of our consideration, at the general assembly to be held on Wednesday the 26th of this month at eleven o'clock precisely, at the Globe Tavern in Fleet-street ; and which meeting I have been principally instrumental in calling.

A plan is struck off, on the other side of this sheet, in order to make the subject more intelligible.

In the summer of 1810, the principal proprietors of the Wilts and Berks Canal projected two lines for the extension of their concern ; the one, from Foxham to Bristol by a line marked (A) the other a junction with the Thames and Severn Canal marked (B) to be called, "THE SEVERN JUNCTION." The Thames and Severn Committee were, very justly, alarmed at the projected line (A) from Foxham, and several conferences were held between the Thames and Severn Committee and the Wilts and Berks proprietors ; the result of which was, a final agreement that the line (A) should be abandoned ; and, that the SEVERN JUNCTION (B) should be adopted ; and, the general assembly of the Thames and Severn Company, having most fully approved and confirmed the proceedings at these conferences, resolved to leave the completion of the matter to their committee.

In consequence of this resolution a Bill was presented to Parliament by the Wilts and Berks company in the Session of 1811 ; and (the terms of junction being settled) the Thames and Severn Canal company presented a petition to the House of Commons praying, that that Bill might pass into a Law.

50

In the course of proceeding it was found that, as alterations in the Thames and Severn Company's Acts would be necessary, it would be proper that the Thames and Severn company should apply for a Bill *of their own*, to go hand in hand with the Severn Junction Bill; in order to effect which, certain previous notices were, by the rules of the House of Commons, necessary; but the time for giving these having expired the Bill was dropped for the Session.

During the summer of 1811, new notices were given, and all other measures necessary, were taken to enable the proprietors of the Severn Junction to re-present their Bill, in the ensuing Session of 1812; and proceedings were had by the *Thames and Severn Company* to enable *them* likewise to go on with their concurrent bill.

Thus stood the negotiation early in January 1812; both parties ready to apply to Parliament for one common object; having, up to that time, the consent of the two concerns.

On the 7th January last, a general assembly of our company was held for the purpose of considering the mode of proceeding with the proposed junction; the expediency of which had been, in the preceding Session, decided upon. At that meeting one of the commissioners of the Thames attended; and stated that a bill was about to be presented to Parliament for the improvement of that river, between Abingdon and the Thames and Severn Canal, at Lechlade; a measure, (if it *had* existed) greatly beneficial to our concern. Upon this statement, those who were present, (except myself) entered into a resolution, " That the proprietors " of the Thames and Severn Canal do not, at present, perceive any ne- " cessity for a junction with the Wilts and Berks at Latton, and therefore " judge it *now* not expedient to consent thereto."

There were present only *two* Proprietors of our Company who are *acting members* of the Committee, besides myself; and *they* did not vote on the question at all; it was supported, by some gentlemen who had come to town on purpose, but whom I do not recollect to have seen more than once before, at any meeting of the Company during the twelve years I have been in the habit of constantly attending them. In fairness to these gentlemen, (for I assume that they must have the interest of the Company at heart) I must say, I believe they were not aware of the nature of the case; or, I think it impossible for them to have supported a motion which has involved us in so much difficulty, such certain expence, and what may be attended ultimately with such ruinous consequences. My earnest endeavours were exerted, in vain, to oppose it.

In consequence of the above assertion of the Thames Commis-sioner, as soon as the time for presenting petitions for private bills was elapsed, I caused the *register of the private bill office* in the House of Com-mons to be searched, and NO PETITION FOR ANY SUCH BILL is to be found.

The natural consequence of so sudden and unexpected turn in politics of the company, was, that the promoters of the Severn Junction disgusted with this apparent versatility and bad faith of the Thames and Severn Canal Company (for such I am sorry to say it is considered by them) have given up their project as far as relates to us.

The Wilts and Berks Company wishing to improve their canal, and hav. g large property in the forest of Dean, in *stone and coal mines*, they ar.

desirous of having a communication with the *upper parts of the Severn*, and finding that we have thus excluded them from obtaining that communication by *our* means they have sought a mode of doing it *without us*.

They have, therefore projected the line (C), from Foxham to Berkley a measure pregnant with the most destructive consequences to *us*, and calling upon us for opposition to the last shilling of our resources.

Under these circumstances, several individual members, holding or representing 747 shares, met last Friday (the 14th); and being convinced that the above resolution of Jan. 7th will be detrimental to the interests of the Thames and Severn canal, they have called a general meeting of the Company as above stated, for the purpose of reconsidering it and determining what may be necessary to be done in consequence.

I sincerely believe, from all the information which I have been laboriously collecting for the last three years, that the SEVERN JUNCTION will be a most beneficial measure for the THAMES AND SEVERN CANAL; the facts within my own knowledge, and that of many members of our Committee, and which I shall have the honor of laying before the general assembly, will, I trust, conjoined to an inspection of the plan, satisfy every unprejudiced proprietor that our property, in this concern, must not only be much deteriorated, but perhaps annihilated, if we do not obtain a canal navigation, to Abingdon IN AID OF THE *partial and interrupted navigation on the River Thames.*

In this view of the subject, it seems important that the Company should reconsider the resolution, which condemned a measure they, last year, so much approved; and that now the matter should be referred to the Committee (as it was last year) for the purpose of reviving the negotiation with the proprietors of the Severn Junction which, I am induced to believe, may be done with effect and advantage to both.

Intreating you will have the goodness to attend at the proposed Meeting, and give us your assistance in replacing our affairs in the situation they were in three months ago when the value of the shares was gradually improving, or that you will intrust your proxies to some friend on whose unbiassed judgment you can rely.

I have the honour to be,

Lincoln's-Inn Fields.
Feb. 18, 1812,

Your humble Servant,
JOHN DISNEY Jun.

J. Office, Printer, Crown-court, Fleet-street.

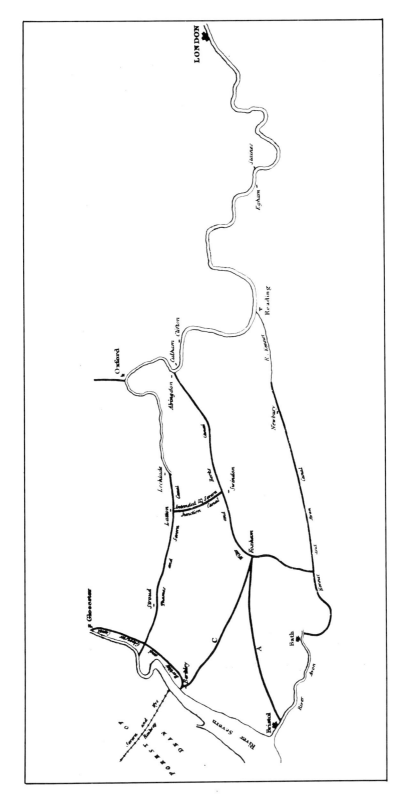

53

either canal. It was agreed that the project should go ahead and be renamed "The North Wilts Canal" (NW). Whitworth's survey and estimate were accepted, the W & B subscribing five twelfths of the cost, the public four and the T & S three twelfths. The meeting then adjourned to the same place on 28th October.

When, at this later meeting, the T & S formally agreed to the junction, Lovenden strode up to the Clerk, John Lane, snatched the minute book from his hands and struck his name out of the list of those present, declaring that he would not have his name appear when he did not approve the resolution.[8]

A Petition to introduce the NW Bill was presented to the House of Commons on 18th December, 1812 and on the same day the T & S asked for a Bill to allow them to complete the canal by making an additional cut to join and communicate with it. This application almost came to grief in February 1813 when the Committee examining it reported that no map, book of reference or list of landowners had been deposited. The basin for which permission was sought was only 192 ft by 60 ft and the maps etc should have been deposited by the NW petitioners. One can imagine the frantic preparation of these papers, which the T & S supplied early in March. Both Bills received the Royal Assent on 2nd July, 1814.[14]

A Petition in support of the NW Bill from "several Gentlemen, Traders and other inhabitants of Cricklade and neighbourhood" has been preserved; it is dated 2nd January, 1813 and has 45 signatures.

The text closely resembles the preamble to the Act (53 Geo. 111 Cap. 182) which stated that

> the canal will greatly facilitate and render more convenient than at present, the conveyance of all kinds of commodities to and from the Towns near the line of such canal and will open a communication between South Wales and the Counties of Hereford and Gloucester and His Majesty's Forest of Dean, and the City of London.[15]

The "Proprietors of the North Wilts Canal Navigation" could take water locally only during construction; they were not to take any from the T & S nor from any of the sources of the Thames. As all water used was to be supplied by the W & B double stop gates were to be fitted within 200 yards of that canal; these could be closed if the W & B, after inspection, were not satisfied that the NW were using water economically. The W & B were to be paid for all water supplied and could appoint three agents to take care of the NW locks. Another stop gate was to be fitted within 100 yards of the junction with the T & S who were to have powers to prevent passage when the NW water was lower than that of their canal. The Proprietors were empowered to raise £60,000 amongst themselves in £25 shares; if this amount was not sufficient another £30,000 could be raised either by the same means or by Mortgage or Promissory Notes. Work was not to commence until £44,000 had been subscribed. Tolls were to be the same as those taken by the W & B but those on goods between Cricklade and the T & S were to be reduced to one half. The Proprietors were to build an aqueduct at least 8 ft wide and 7 ft high over the River Churn and four other arches of similiar size under the canal in the lands of John Lord Eliot to carry off flood water.

The list of subscribers was deposited in the Office of the Clerk of the Peace

Intended NORTH WILTS CANAL.

THE Act for making the Thames and Severn Canal was passed in the year 1783, and the Canal has been finished upwards of twenty-five years, forming a Water Communication between the River Severn and the Thames. This Communication was considered of great public advantage, and promised well to the Subscribers, who expended upon it upwards of two hundred and fifty thousand pounds: but it has been rendered next to useless, in consequence of the bad state of the Thames from Leachlade to Oxford. The Proprietors, however, have from time to time had their hopes and expectations kept up by assurances that the River, between Leachlade and Oxford, would be improved: but after continual disappointments for more than twenty-five years, they now find, that at a Meeting held at Oxford on the 29th day of January last, the Thames Commissioners acknowledged it to be wholly out of their power to improve that part of the Navigation. The public object, therefore, of a Communication between the two Rivers, the Severn and the Thames, will be defeated, and the large sum which has been expended for that purpose lost to the Proprietors, unless some Line from the Thames and Severn Canal, to a more navigable part the River Thames, be formed.

The PROPOSED NORTH WILTS CANAL, which will join the Thames and Severn with the Wilts and Berks Canal, and thus complete a perfect Canal Navigation between the two great Rivers, is the least expensive Communication that can be made, and will realize to the Public the object for which the Thames and Severn Canal was originally made, and, it is hoped, make some return of interest to the Proprietors of that Undertaking for the large sum they have expended.

Beside a loss of interest on two hundred and fifty thousand pounds for twenty-five years, the Concern itself is reduced in public estimation to less than a quarter of the original cost; and as this is wholly owing to the improvement of the River not having been effected between Leachlade and Oxford, which was always held out to the Proprietors of the Thames and Severn Navigation, but is now abandoned, they trust that their situation will receive the serious consideration of the House of Commons; and that as the making of the North Wilts Canal will not only relieve them, but be of great public utility, they rely upon its receiving the sanction of Parliament.

The projected Canal, and also the Thames and Severn, and Wilts and Berks Canals, are delineated on the annexed Plan; a bare inspection of which will shew that the Communication must be advantageous to the Public. It will open an Inland Navigation between the Cities of Gloucester, Worcester, Hereford, and London; and be the best Line of Conveyance to the Metropolis for the Iron, Copper, and Tin of South Wales; and for the valuable Products of the Forest of Dean, where the finest Timber for the Navy is grown.

An opposition to this Canal is expected from some Public Bodies interested in other Communications; but the grounds of their opposition being averse to the public interest, prove the utility of the North Wilts Canal, and, the Promoters of it presume, will forward, rather than obstruct, its reception by Parliament.

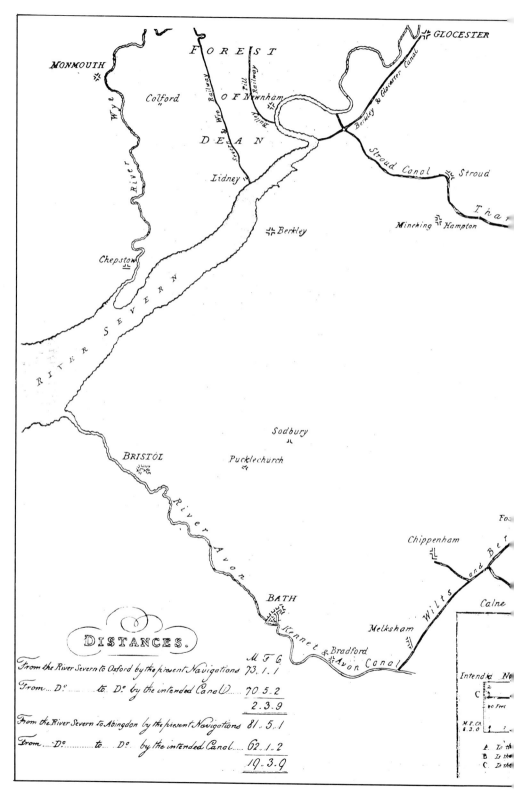

GLOCESTER

FOREST

MONMOUTH

Colford

OF Newnham

Wye Railway

Berkley & Glocester Canal

Till Railway

Riling Railway

DEAN

Stroud Canal

Stroud

Lidney

Tha

River Wye

Berkley

Minching Hampton

Chepstow

RIVER SEVERN

Sodbury

BRISTOL

Pucklechurch

Fo

Chippenham

River Avon

Calne

BATH

Wilts and Ber

Kennet

Melksham

& Bradford

Avon Canal

Intended N

C

40 Feet

M.F.Ch.
4. 3. 0   1

A. Is the

B. Is the

C. Is the

Plan OF Navigations Connected with the Intended NORTH WILTS CANAL, 1813

Cirencester

Severn

Latton Canal

Lechlade

Cricklade

Buscot

Radcot

Ensham

Intended North Wilts Canal

Blundsdon

Highworth

Faringdon

River

Thames

Wilts

Shrivenham

Longcot

Kingston Inn

Swindon

and

Canal

Abingdon

Berks Canal

Wantage

Sutton Courtney

SECTION.

Wilts Canal   B   Wilts   and   Berks   Canal   A

Scale of Miles

of the Wilts & Berks Canal with the River Thames at Abingdon.
of the same Canal with the intended North Wilts Canal, being a Rise of 168 feet from the Thames at Abingdon.
of the intended Canal with the Thames & Severn Canal, which is 58.8 fall from the Wilts & Berks.

in the County of Wilts on 14th September, 1813, together with a plan, elevations of the main aqueducts to be built, a sectional plan showing the location and fall of the 11 locks and also a list of the owners or occupiers of lands to be crossed.

The total sum advanced was £44,750 from 116 subscribers. By far the greatest amount came from Proprietors of the W&B over and above that Company's £15,000. The Earl of Peterborough provided £5,500, the Morlands £1,700, Nathaniel Atherton £1,250, William Hallett £1,000, John Prower £800, James Crowdy £750, Joseph Priestley £700, William Whitworth £500 and Ambrose Goddard £225. Seven T&S Proprietors subscribed £1,900 of which the Disney family contributed £1,000. Thirty subscribers from Oxford produced nearly £6,000, six from Abingdon £1,400 and seventeen from London £3,000. The Bullo Pill Railway Company provided £500 and the T&S subscribed the £5,000 allowed in their Bill.[16] This sum had been agreed by the T&S when Disney reported in October 1812 at a NW Subscribers meeting where he stated that because of delays many subscribers had withdrawn their support and unless the two Companies subscribed in their Corporate capacity the project would have to be abandoned for lack of funds. The meeting had resolved that as the junction would provide a profit to them of £2,000 a year (nearly equal to their net revenue at that time), £5,000, the amount of their sinking fund, should be advanced together with £250 towards the expenses of the application to Parliament.[2]

On 24th February 1814 Disney and Lane met Whitworth and Crowdy at Latton; they saw Lord Eliot's stewards and marked out the outline of the basin.[2]

Friction developed between the Companies during the building of the junction. Whitworth had asked that the position of the basin should be altered to avoid an awkward aqueduct over the Thames. The T&S had agreed to this but the question then arose as to who should pay for the aqueduct now needed to cross the River Churn which flowed between the basin and the T&S. Counsel's opinion was sought in July, this stated that as the T&S first occupied the ground by making the basin they could not compel the NW to make the aqueduct, that canal now ending at the point of junction with the basin and not being continued to the Churn. The Acts were defective, neither Company could be compelled to make the aqueduct and it was doubtful if the T&S had powers to build it unless by arrangement with the NW or people connected with the river.[17]

The T&S finally built it under the supervision of John Denyer, their Manager. Two estimates were obtained; if an iron cylinder were used the cost would be £230, a more conventional stone structure would cost £311. The latter was chosen.[18]

The remainder of the NW was built under the supervision of William Whitworth. It included a 100 yard tunnel at Cricklade and three small aqueducts following earlier Brindley designs and consisting of embankments through the bottom of which rivers flowed in three low culverts.

Loveden watched the building in a mood of gloomy foreboding; in a letter of 2nd November he writes ". . . the North Wilts is a bad prospect and proceeds very slowly."[7] By 1817 work had virtually ceased owing to lack of funds; application was then made to the Exchequer Loan Commissioners for

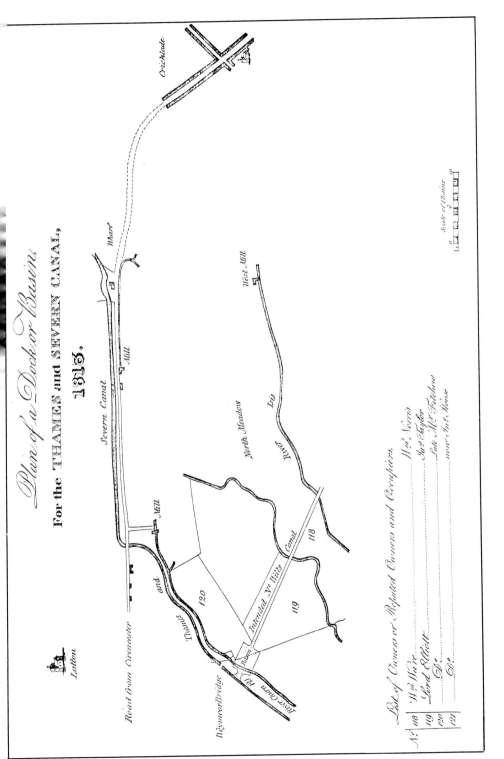

Plan of a Dock or Basin,

For the THAMES and SEVERN CANAL,

1815.

Cricklade

Wharf

Severn Canal

Mill

West Mill

North Meadow

River Iris

Latton

Road from Cirencester

Thames and

Mill

120

Intended No. Wilts Canal

118

119

Basin

Newman Bridge

River Churn (d.)

List of Owners or Reputed Owners and Occupiers

No.		
118	Wm Warr	Wm Norris
119	Lord Elliott	Jas Taylor
120	Do.	Late Mr Fletcher
121	Do.	now Mr. House

Scale of Chains

59

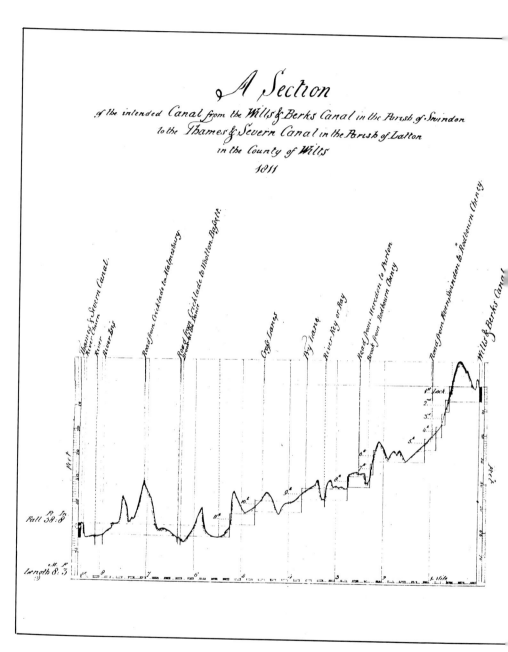

A Section

of the intended Canal from the Wilts & Berks Canal in the Parish of Swindon
to the Thames & Severn Canal in the Parish of Latton
in the County of Wilts

1811

the money necessary to complete the line. This Commission was set up under the 1817 Poor Employment Act "for the carrying on of Public works and Fisheries, and the employment of the poor in manner therein." The Commissioners agreed to lend £24,000 at 5 per cent interest but only £15,000 was taken, £6,000 in March 1818, £6,000 later that year and £3,000 in 1819.[17]

John Denyer wrote to J.S. Salt the T&S Treasurer on 21st January, 1817

> The traffic from Brimscombe to London is almost nil. I hope to see the North Wilts proceeded with in the spring, the completion of which I have not the slightest doubt will materially improve our Tonnage.

On 25th August, 1818 he reported that work at Latton was under way and on 8th September

> The North Wilts is to go ahead, having got a loan from the Exchequer Commissioners.[19]

Tolls of £26 were collected during May 1818 but the canal was not officially opened, without fuss, until 2nd April, 1819. Priestley marvels that it cost less than the estimated price of £60,000, the actual cost being the £44,750 subscribed plus the £15,000 borrowed.

The NW Proprietors were in financial difficulties almost at once; during the first seven weeks of operation their tolls were only £150.[20] At the end of the first year they could not repay the first instalment due to the Exchequer Loan Commissioners and proposed incorporation with the W&B who had little option but to agree that this was very much in their interests. In February 1820 they petitioned for a Bill to unite the two canals. "The Petitioners as a body, being considerable shareholders in the North Wilts and the two navigations being so interwoven and connected with each other as to regulations of trade and supply of water, apprehend that it would be beneficial and expedient to incorporate the two." The preamble to the resulting Act (2 Geo. IV Cap. 97) summarised the W&B and NW Acts and stated that both canals had been made except for the reservoirs and several of the feeders. As most of the Proprietors were common to both Companies it would be highly expedient and beneficial to unite the affairs and concerns of the two undertakings and as an agreement had been made the two Acts should be repealed and the powers, provisions and authorities of the same considered in one Act. All conveyances were to be transferred to the United Company and the powers to make reservoirs and to take water from Wanborough Brook were reserved. The rules governing both Companies were restated and were to be those of the United Navigations. No actions already brought were to be abated by the Act.[21]

The W&B took over the Exchequer debt which was paid off by February 1836.[17]

In 1821 Edward Protheroe was sending 18 boat loads of Forest coal from Brimscombe down to the W&B but at the same time William Quarrell of Cricklade and the Stranges of Swindon were carrying Somerset coal up to Cricklade despite the fact that Forest coal was charged one shilling per ton and Somerset coal two shillings per ton. The canal never came up to the expectations of the Forest coal concerns. During the later years for which records are available (1838–1862), with one exception, twice as much coal passed into the T&S from the W&B as came from that line. In 1840 over 15,000 tons of Forest coal poured down the NW for use in the building of the Great Western Railway. In a letter to the T&S written in 1828, Dunsford, the W&B manager, stated that Forest coal was never popular on that line for household use.[22]

References

1   K&A minute book 10 July 1803.
2   TS 164a&c Blacks reports.
3   TS 207 20/3.
4   GCL JF 14 54 11.
5   WRO 109/900/910.
6   GCL JV14 1.
7   Thacker, The Thames Highway.
8   TS 166.
9   GCL JV 14 1.
10   TS 207 20/4.
11   BRO D EEL 07.
12   TS 207 20/4.
13   JHC Vol 66 p37–230.
14   JHC Vol 68 p91–592.
15   WRO 54/129.
16   WRO List of NW subscribers.
17   TS 193/22 and SRL D1–3.
18   TS 164C Aug 29 1816.
19   TS 220.
20   TS 207/15.
21   JHC Vol 76 p49–411.
22   SRL letter book.

Chapter Seven
The Years of near Prosperity 1817–1841

On the departure of Joseph Priestley early in 1817 William Dunsford was appointed Superintendent. As an employee of the Oxford Canal Company he had been active in plotting against W&B opposition at Abingdon; he was no less active as W&B manager in opposing his old Company. He was a prolific letter writer and copies of these written between 1824 and 1839, luckily preserved, shed much light on canal business and politics. Very little is known of his life apart from his canal work. William Corbett in his *Rural Rides* mentions the W&B, though not by name, and Dunsford's Swindon home in 1826.

> Just before we got to Swindon we crossed a canal at a place where there is a wharf and a coal-yard, and close by these a Gentleman's house, with coach-house, stable, walled-in garden, paddock orné, and the rest of those things, which, all together, make up a villa, surpassing the second, and approaching the first class. Seeing a man in the coal-yard I asked him to what gentleman the house belonged; "To the head un o' the canal" said he. And, when, upon further enquiry of him, I found that it was the villa of the chief manager, I could not help congratulating the proprietors of this aquatic concern, for, though I did not ask the name of the canal, I could readily suppose the profits must be prodigious, when the residence of the manager, would imply no disparagement of dignity, if occupied by a Secretary of State for the Home or even for the Foreign department. I mean an English Secretary of State; for as to an American one, his salary would be wholly inadequate to a residence in a mansion like this.

Cobett was wrong about the canal profits which were never prodigious. Dunsford's private activities as a trader in coal and stone later gave rise to suspicions that he manipulated canal tolls etc. for his own benefit; this may account for Cobett's enthusiasm. Many years later Dunsford's house was occupied by G.J. Churchward, from 1902 to 1921 the Chief Mechanical Engineer of the Great Western Railway.

In 1816 the W&B, experiencing a shortage of water on the summit level, and faced with the prospect of having to supply the NW, then under construction, undertook, without adequate geological advice, the digging of a well north of Swindon to tap underground supplies. This well reached a depth of about 120ft and a boring continued another 120ft down without success. William Smith, the father of English geology and one time surveyor of the SCC, was asked for advice. His report, dated 13th April, 1816, stated that his study of the local strata indicated that below the 240ft of clay already pierced there was a 20 to 30ft layer of oolite rock with water underneath.

Digging continued and at 261ft, the last 15ft through rock, uprushing water filled 15 to 18ft of the well with sand brought from below the limestone rock, and the assistance of a steam engine was required to prosecute the still incomplete experiment. In December the level of water rising through a 3 inch borehole reached 70ft in 26 hours and the ultimate success of the scheme appeared probable but by 1820 the supply of water was found to be very limited and the experiment was abandoned.[2]

Edward Protheroe, whom we have already seen to have extensive interests in the Forest of Dean wrote to Dunsford on 26th August, 1820; "You informed me that the W & B had other means of procuring water after their steam engine had failed, and I am persuaded that they cannot too soon adopt these means if they look to an extension of trade to the Thames."[3]

In a letter which accompanied the notice of the general meeting of 12th January, 1821 James Crowdy stated that trade had been steadily increasing since 1815 to May 1820, all profits being devoted to liquidating debts, improving works and particularly in endeavouring to provide, by purchasing every stream within the power of the Act, an adequate supply of water, but the experience of the last summer had shown that the resources were still insufficient and the decrease of the last years trade was entirely due to this. The Committee had determined to build the reservoir at Coate empowered in the Act, this would afford the necessary supply in the dry season and without it the Concern could never be regarded as complete.[4]

One wonders why the estimates and frequent assurances of the Whit-worths had gone so sadly astray; Robert's earlier experience on the T & S should have been a warning and William was strangely silent on the matter.

The meeting passed the resolution "That the immediate construction of Coate reservoir under the Authority of the original Act is indispensibly necessary for the adequate supply of water to support the increasing trade." £10,000, the estimated cost, was raised by £3 shares; plans had already been prepared the previous year. A bank 22 ft high was to be built at the northern end of the valley, a dam in the south east branch and earth embankments elsewhere. The culvert stipulated in the Act for returning unwanted water to its original course was built of brick and was 4 ft in diameter. Richard Jefferies in his *History of Swindon* tells of difficulties with the building of this culvert.

This valley (of Coate) was enclosed by a bank at each extremity, and the water of a brook which originally ran through it, together with that from other springs artificially compelled to run here, being allowed to accumulate, formed exactly what was desired; while the original course of the brook took off any superfluity that might occur from flooding, and by a branch from it the canal could always be supplied. But the site offered one difficulty. There was a spring rising immediately without the upper bank of the reservoir, which it was found impossible to make run into it; moreover it was wanted by the farmers and inhabitants of the vale beneath. A brick culvert was accordingly constructed but an unfortunate oversight occurred. That part of the bottom of the reservoir over which it was necessary the culvert should be carried at the latter end of its course, had originally been but one remove from a morass, in short, was very shaky. Upon this unstable foundation the culvert seems to have been placed, and with the result which might have been anticipated. The weight of the brickwork, with a superincumbent load of earth and sand thrown on, proved too great for the soft ooze upon which it was placed. The culvert gradually sank in places, the brickwork cracked and leaks have ever since been more or less frequent. One occurred of a very serious character when the meadows below were flooded by the escaped water of the reservoir and had not a hatch been beaten down by sledge hammers, it has been thought the reservoir bank must have been washed away, and the thousands of tons of water it contained would have been precipitated into the vale, the effect of which would have been an enormous damage to property and probable loss of life.

The first conveyances of land were made in 1821, the work being com-

The Kennet and Avon Locks at Semington with the entrance of the Wilts and Berks Canal under the Bridge on the left.

The walled off entrance and Toll Collectors Cottage at Semington, photographed in 1970.

A fine view of narrow boat FAITH (c.1900) with Mr John Trow at the tiller and Mr W.H. Brinkworth standing. Seen here at Chippenham Wharf, now the site of the Bus Station. This barge normally carried coal from Camerton in Somerset to Chippenham, taking two days to do so.

A Period Piece! The Lift Bridge at Rey Mill, Lacock c.1900.

The remains of Stanley Aqueduct seen from both sides in 1970, the top photograph shows west and bottom, east.

Top Lock of the "Seven Locks" showing the bottom Gates photographed in 1970.

A busy scene at Vastern Wharf on the Wilts and Berks Canal.

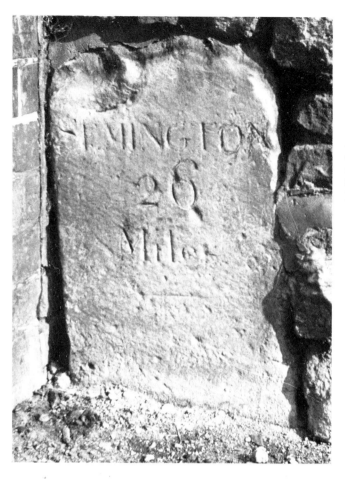

A canal milestone. This was displaced by the construction of the Brunel Centre, Swindon and is now in "The Parade".

The junction of the Wilts and Berks Main line and the North Wilts Canal in Swindon seen here from 1914 from the Golden Lion Bridge.

Junction of the Main Line and the North Wilts Canal seen from Whale Bridge with the Golden Lion Bridge seen ahead in 1914.

On the Main Line Section in Swindon. Malborough Road footbridge in the distance photographed in 1914.

Drove Road Bridge seen here in 1914 with Swindon Wharf in the background, looking East.

Swindon Wharf, looking from Drove Road Bridge in 1914.

John Street Bridge and a section of the North Wilts Canal in Swindon photographed in 1914.

A fine period view, with children catching butterflies at Rodbourne Road Bridge on the North Wilts Canal with Swindon Lock under the bridge, photographed 1914.

Looking West from Chaddington Lane Bridge with Summit Lock Cottage in the distance, c.1970. The bridge is now demolished.

Already derelict in 1914. A view of Summit Lock.

Summit Lock in 1899 with the lock keepers house in the background with his family on parade.

The boat "DRAGONFLY" photographed here in 1895 at the Ardington Top Lock. Note the photographer's bag in the lower left of the picture.

The overgrown chamber of Ardington Top Lock in 1970.

Abingdon Basin, c.1900 with Caldecot Road footbridge in the distance.

The Wilts and Berks Canal bridge over the River Ock in Abingdon.

"Abingdon by Moonlight", painted by Henry Pether (1828–1865) showing the entrance to the Wilts and Berks Canal near to St. Helen's Wharf, c.1860.

Hunter's Bridge just north of Wantage, with a "lone rower".

Wantage Wharf, c.1900.

The South portal of Cricklade Tunnel on the North Wilts Canal seen here in 1970, now buried and built over.

Moredon Aqueduct which carried the North Wilts Canal over the River Ray.

pleted by 1822, but not without the usual difficulties apart from the one described above. On 22nd October there was a report "Workmen are at a standstill because they cannot enter Mr Wynham's land at Coate." The surface area of the completed reservoir was 52¼ acres and the capacity 122 million gallons. Water was fed to the canal just east of Swindon by a long open ditch across a two mile stretch of low meadowland; the plan book at Swindon includes a large scale map of this feeder.

The W&B was unable to compete with the K&A for through Bristol to London trade. In a letter to an Oxford enquirer Dunsford explains why.

> As far as cost is concerned the W&B could compete with the K&A. Although they charge the full rate on W&B trade, the Abingdon barge masters as content to work for a very low rate. But in time the K&A undertakes delivering in nine days whereas the W&B, even if it had regular establishments in London and Bristol could not be less than three weeks, the delay being on the Thames. Both canals are beaten in price by the coastal trade where time does not matter.[5]

The W&B had been liberally sprinkled with wooden drawbridges, these being a continual source of trouble. Writing in answer to a complaint about delay in having one repaired Dunsford writes

> I cannot refrain from saying that I consider all timber bridges on canals as extremely objectionable as they ought never to be resorted to (and I believe never are) except from want of means to build more durable ones. The state of the wretched things bearing the name of bridges on this canal after a wear of not more than 30 years fully bears out this dictum, and I trust I am doing my duty in substituting brick or stone wherever it is practicable.[6]

A letter of 17th January, 1825 makes the first reference to possible competition from a railway; Dunsford shrugs this off by saying that he was not aware of any projected railway that was likely to injure the W&B except the one from Bristol to London, but as no details of this project were available no opinion could be formed as to the line. This letter also describes how the large Proprietors had decided that no dividend should be paid until all debts had been cleared and improvements to the wharves completed. The decrease in tolls for 1824 was due to bad harvests in the Vale of Berks and two months floods on the Thames which had reduced the coal trade between Abingdon and Reading.

The story of the struggle to increase trade in coal by pleading, bullying and stealth is best told by a selection of Dunsford's letters; these are presented in a separate chapter.

Early in 1826 he first refers to the experiment of running a small fast boat service by Franklin and Parker, two Witney traders, between Gloucester and London using the Gloucester and Berkeley, Stroudwater, T&S, and the W&B from Latton to Abingdon. These small "fly boats" had been in service for some years on many other canals. They were lightly built with a sharp prow and could carry up to 15 tons; they were hauled by relays of horses, travelling by day and night and being given priority of passage. Similiar, but even lighter boats were in use on the Glasgow, Paisley and Ardrossan canal for passenger transport; these were light wooden boats with steel frames and a keel for easier steering. They carried 80–100 passengers at 10 m.p.h. when hauled by a pair of horses, each pair covering 4 miles between changes.[7]

REDUCED PRICE OF CARRIAGE,

BY THE

Wilts and Berks
CANAL COMPANY,

TO AND FROM

London and Bristol.

BOATS will set out weekly, with or without a full Freight, from the *Three Cranes and Hambro' Wharfs*, Queen Street, LONDON, and from the *Wilts and Berks Wharf*, Temple Back, BRISTOL.

By this Conveyance Goods will be forwarded with dispatch, to and fro' between BRISTOL and LONDON, and the intervening Places:

AT THE FOLLOWING PRICES: .

	Price of Carriage of the following Articles.			
	Goods and Merchandize per Ton.	Corn per Quarter.		
		Pease and Beans.	Wheat.	Barley and Oats.
	£. s. d.	s. d.	s. d.	s. d.
BRISTOL to the Wilts and Berks Canal Wharf Sydney Gardens, BATH	0 8 4	1 10	1 8	1 5
———to Melksham and Lacock	0 16 0	3 3	3 0	2 6
———to Chippenham and Calne	1 0 0	3 10	3 6	3 0
———to Dantsey	1 0 0	4 0	3 7	3 0
———to Wootton-Basset	1 0 6	4 2	3 9	3 1
———to Swindon	1 1 6	4 11	4 4	3 5
———to Longcot Wharf near Farringdon	1 2 6	5 4	4 9	3 11
———to Wantage	1 4 0	5 6	5 0	4 1
———to Abingdon	1 5 0	6 0	5 6	4 6
BRISTOL to LONDON	2 2 0	9 4	8 5	7 0
LONDON to Abingdon	1 5 0	4 0	3 8	3 0
———to Wantage	1 5 0	4 8	4 6	3 6
———to Longcot Wharf near Farringdon	1 7 0	5 2	4 10	4 0
———to Swindon	1 9 0	5 7	5 2	4 3
———to Wootton-Basset	1 11 6	5 10	5 4	4 5
———to Dantsey	1 12 6	5 11	5 5	4 6
———to Chippenham, Calne, Lacock, and Melksham	1 13 6	6 3	5 9	4 8
———to Bath	1 15 0	8 0	7 2	5 10
LONDON to BRISTOL	2 2 0	8 9	8 5	7 0
ABINGDON to Wantage	0 5 0	1 0	0 10	0 8
———to Longcot	0 7 0	1 3	1 2	1 0
———to Swindon	0 9 0	1 7	1 6	1 3
———to Wootton-Basset	0 11 6	2 2	1 11	1 7
———to Dantsey	0 12 6	2 5	2 2	1 9
———to Chippenham, Calne, and Melksham	0 13 6	3 3	2 11	2 5
———to Bath	0 16 8	4 0	3 6	2 10
———to Bristol	1 5 0	5 10	5 2	4 3

Wharfs where Goods are received, and Wharfingers Names.

LONDON,	Three Cranes and Hambro' Wharfs,	Messrs. SILLS, RAMSAY, and GRAY.
ABINGDON,	Canal Wharf,	MR. J. PRINCE.
WANTAGE,	Ditto	MR. S. PLUMB.
LONGCOT,	Ditto	MR. J. CARTER.
SWINDON,	Ditto	MR. J. CANN.
WOOTTON-BASSET,	Ditto	MR. J. GARDINER.
DANTSEY,	Ditto	Messrs. HOPKINS.
CALNE,	Ditto	MR. ATCHLEY.
CHIPPENHAM,	Ditto	MR. WHARRY.
LACOCK,	Ditto	MR. C. PETTIFER.
MELKSHAM,	Ditto	MR. D. MULCOCK.
BATH,	Sydney Wharf,	MR. R. CLARKE.
BRISTOL,	Wilts and Berks Wharf, Temble Backs,	MR. T. HOWE.

N. B. Goods intended for Oxford, Witney, Banbury, Burford, and other parts of the North of England, are regularly forwarded from Abingdon.

☞ There are regular Passage Boats twice a Week, from the Canal Wharf, ABINGDON, to the Wilts and Berks Wharf, Sydney Gardens, BATH.

Dunsford was in favour of the Gloucester-London service but had to fight hard to get the T&S to agree to charge tonnage sufficiently low to make it economic to the trader. The first mention of this service in the latter's records occurs on 27th October, 1829 when a special committee meeting was held at Brimscombe, the service starting officially on 1st November. In December Dunsford was still arguing with the T&S,

> Mr Parker would be quite satisfied if the tonnage on all articles passing our two canals was reduced to two shillings and sixpence per ton, and seeing as I do the great exertions he is making and the loss he is at present sustaining I really think we ought not to stand out about trifles. I consider that if there are some articles on which the Carrier can charge the Consumer a higher rate, that it is a bonus which we ought not to grudge him or wish to participate in, we should remember that we know the extent of our sacrifice while he is exposed to various risks and contingin-cies. I am aware that wool which was one of the commodities excepted in Mr Denyer's tariff is bulky and light, but when I see boats passing with 3 or 4 tons only, and perseveringly keeping their times to a certain loss, I am inclined to except even this. Let us get the wool and everything else off the roads and on our canals; let our boats work with the regularity of Pickfords and show the Public that the thing is to be done, and then if we see that Mr Parker is getting more then his share, we can easily increase our dues.

Pickfords were early and widespread canal carriers who operated until forced to withdraw by railway competition about 1847.

An agreement was finally reached that all goods should be carried on both canals at a flat rate of two shillings and sixpence per ton. The service was popular on account of its speed and regularity, the average transit time from London to Gloucester being 6 days and the return one day less. In the first year of operation the through traffic had been trebled and by 1834 it had risen by six times. But it was still not economic either to the canal Companies or the Carriers. The three firms involved, Parker and Foster, George Franklin and Bowerman Son and Mason were in financial trouble by 1833, both the T&S and the W&B having difficulty in getting their accounts settled. In that year the T&S considered that they could no longer afford the low tonnage on bulkier materials and issued a notice to the Carriers telling them that from 27th April, 1834 the rate on these goods would be increased to four shillings per ton. To obtain the concession of decreased tolls all fly boats had to be registered.[8] The Carriers wisely refrained from telling Dunsford of this increase and it was not until October that he learnt of it. His reaction was as might be expected.

> I saw Parker yesterday and he informs me that the T&S have since April last increased their tonnage on some part of the fly boat trade. As it was an understood principle from the commencement of this Trade that the two Companies were to act in unison as to their charges, I am quite certain that the W&B Company would not have made the smallest alteration thereof, for it must be obvious that if any part of the Trade will bear an additional impost it ought to be shared by both the Parties, who, having established it by a concurrent reduction of their Parliamentary rate, should equally participate in any increase which can be prudently and fairly obtained. From a person less accurate in matters of business than Mr Parker I own I should have doubted the truth of the information – at least I should have suspected some misrepresentation capable of satisfactory explanation – but his positive assur-ance of the facts leaves me no alternative than to request you will be good enough,

at your earliest convenience, to acquaint me with the articles on which for the last six months the additional toll has been charged, and perhaps you will also state, for the information of our Committee, why they were not favoured with some notice of the intentions of the T&S when they determined to make so material an alteration in the original agreement.[9]

Denyer replied that the increase was not secret as six months notice had been given omitting to mention that the notice had only given to the Carriers who in their wisdom had not told Dunsford fearing that he too might increase his toll. Denyer listed the trade surcharged as:

Bowerman & Son	466 tons 10 cwt.	
Allen & Mason	88	15
Parker & Foster	216	7

and the total collected in extra tolls was £57.17s.0d. Notice the regrouping of the Companies, George Franklin is not included; his business had been taken over by Bowerman who was himself later absorbed by Parker.

The T&S finally agreed to refund the surcharge, the W&B considering that the Carriers should not be forced to pay them a similiar amount, they having difficulty enough in coping with the Thames. The T&S minutes of a meeting of 28th April, 1835 records their climb down, but in a face saving manner,

> The increased fly boat tonnage does not appear to operate beneficially to the Interests of this Canal, and is considered by the W&B as not in accordance with the undertaking made with that Company in September 1829. Resolved, to reduce the toll to two shillings and sixpence per ton, and to make a further reduction of 6d per ton on all kinds of iron and nails carried beyond Whitchurch on the Thames. Also resolved, to take measures in conjunction with the W&B to reduce the size of certain locks.

We will consider this last later in connection with the 1835 W&Act.

Between 1st November, 1829 and 28th June, 1834 the total revenue paid by the Carriers running the fly boat service was £1,483.17s.0d for 12,144 tons of merchandise carried in 1,621 boat passages at an average toll of 18s.3d.[10] Traffic continued to grow; in 1839 372 boats carried 5,162 tons and the tolls had risen to £1.14s.0d per passage.[11]

In 1840 the W&B was swamped by the traffic involved in the building of the GWR; when the fury had died down all trade declined except that in Somerset coal. The choice of Swindon as their chief engineering works for that railway was partly influenced by the presence there of the W&B. Daniel Gooch wrote to Brunel stating that Swindon would a suitable location, "The Wilts and Berks canal there would allow coal and coke to be obtained at a moderate price, the canal and its reservoir would also serve in the last resort as a water supply."[1]

We must now retrace our path back to 1831. In that year the payment of dividends was resumed. Dunsford had earlier written, "The Optional Note debt is now liquidated and every Tradesman's bill that could be got in has been discharged so that the Company has no simple contract debt of the slightest consequence."[12] The first dividend distributed was £4,000, the amount rose steadily to a maximum of £9,000 in 1840 and 1841 and then tapered away to the final payment of £561 in 1870.

HAMBRO' WHARF.

(Adjoining The Iron Bridge.)

PARKER & FOSTER having determined to work *their own Boats throughout*, hereby respectfully inform the Public, that their FLY BOATS will ply as stated below, and they are resolved that nothing but unavoidable impediments in the Navigation shall cause delay, and if such should occur, they will (if required) forward the Goods by Land at the customary Rates; but they are pleased at being enabled to acquaint the Public, that the Commissioners of the River Thames intend to persevere and remove all obstructions to the Navigation.

DELIVER GOODS AT

Leave ~bro' Wharf, London.						Arrive at Gloucester.
TUESDAYS ..	Wantage, Faringdon, Highworth Lechlade, Fairford, Quinnington Swindon, Cricklade, & Cirencester	} SATURDAYS.	Chalford, Brimscombe, Stroud, Caincross, Ebley, and Stonehouse,	} MONDAYS	MONDAY
THURSDAYS	......Ditto........Ditto........	TUESDAYS	Ditto........Ditto....	WEDNESDAYS	WEDNESDAYS
SATURDAYS	......Ditto........Ditto........	THURSDAYS	Ditto........Ditto....	FRIDAYS	FRIDAYS

Leave Gloucester.	Leave Briscombe.	Arrive at Hambro' Wharf, London.
MONDAY...............................	MONDAY Evening	...............FRIDAY
WEDNESDAY	WEDNESDAY ditto	...............MONDAY
FRIDAY...............................	FRIDAY ditto	...............WEDNESDAY

Goods conveyed by these Fly Boats to all places on the line of the River Thames, Wilts and Berks, and Thames and Severn Canals; also forwarded to *Cheltenham, Worcestershire, Herefordshire, Monmouthshire,* 1 *North and South Wales.*

69

In June 1832 Nathaniel Atherton of Calne complained of difficulties on that branch due to inadequate maintenance. Dunsford admitted that the locks needed rebuilding but this would involve borrowing £1,500 – £2,000 from the Government and stopping traffic for 6–8 months. This he said was impossible and instead repairs were carried out piecemeal. In the autumn of the same year a general notice was issued to all traders warning them not to load more than 25 tons, only 3½ ft depth could be guaranteed along the main line. These two decisions represent a change of policy, the Company choosing to pay dividends rather than use the money for essential maintenance.

Early in 1833, with railway competition imminent, the K&A, W&B, GJ and Oxford Companies co-operated in trials of a wrought iron boat *Swallow* which was designed to carry passengers and freight at some 8 to 9 m.p.h. On the W&B summit during speed trials she covered 1,560 yards in 4 minutes (13¼ m.p.h.) and later 836 yards in 2 min. 28 sec. (11½ m.p.h.).[13] At these high speeds no injury was done to the canal banks. The technique of lifting the boat up on its bow wave is well described by C.S. Forester in *Hornblower and the Atropos*. *Swallow* was later purchased by the K&A and used on passenger services between Bradford-on-Avon and Bath.

The Great Western Railway promoted a Bill in 1833 for its London to Reading and Bath to Bristol sections; approval for the intermediate length which would directly menace the W&B was to be sought in 1834. The first Bill was rejected in the House of Lords as the result of pressure from land owning interests. Undismayed, the Directors continued to raise additional capital and an Act for the complete line was passed in August 1835 despite objections in which the W&B and K&A had taken active parts, but independently. The K&A chief clerk, Thomas Merriman had written to William Crowdy on 22nd February, 1835,

> The Kennet and Avon Committee will meet next Wednesday for the consideration of Railway affairs, you are no doubt aware of Payne's proposal that a fund of £1,500 should be raised to carry through the general opposition to the GWR Bill – you can inform me how the Wilts and Berks Committee are disposed as to contribution. It appears to me that the line of the GWR would interfere more with your local trade than with ours. We shall be obliged to you for a copy of your proposed Bill.

The prompt reply was

> . . . there does not seem to be much dread of the Railroad and I really cannot say anything about the scheme of contribution to oppose, your letter has conveyed to me the first intimation of such a proposal.[3]

This blindness to the threat posed by the GWR is curious; in 1836 the W&B seemed so sure that their future was safe that they started buying up their own shares, spending £305.10s.0d that year, £648 in 1837 and £429 in 1840.

The W&B Bill referred to received the Royal Assent on 3rd July, 1835 as *5&6 Wm IV Cap. 5a*. It is a peculiar Act in many ways containing as it does provisions for legalising bye-laws which had been in operation for 20 years, admitting that the Longcot branch had been built without authority and finally obtaining permission for the T&S to shorten many of their locks. The Title is "An Act for consolidating the shares in the Wilts and Berks Canal Navigation and for extending the Powers of the Act of Incorporation of the Company of Proprietors of the said Canal." The preamble states that the shares now number 20,000; it is expedient to consolidate these and reduce them to 5,000 representing a Capital of £321,613. Clause 7 states

That the cut or branch from the said canal in the Parish of Shrivenham called the Longcot branch as well as towing path, wharf, warehouses etc (having been made through lands purchased in Trust for the said Company in or about 1807 and having been ever since possessed and used by the said Company although not so made pursuant to the Powers and Directions of the original Act of Incorporation of the said Company) in case the same are not already vested in the said Company by the said recited Act, shall be, and the same are hereby vested and confirmed to the said Company for the same Estate and Interest as the Parties at the time of conveying the same then had therein.

Clauses 13–20 and 22–37 restate the bye-laws in use since 1819. 21 states

Provided always that it shall not be deemed an undue preference in any Toll Collector or Lock keeper of the said Company to permit any boat or vessel usually denominated Fly boats to pass any stop gate, bar or lock at extraordinary hours before a boat or vessel laden with heavy commodities, and not coming under the description of a Fly boat.

This rule too had been in force for many years.

Clause 38 obtains permission for the T&S to carry out modifications to their canal including shortening of locks and other works. This seems a curious way to get these powers; presumably they made some financial arrangements with the W&B to include this clause, thus saving themselves the expense of a separate Bill. The T&S were slow in using this power because such alterations would permanently exclude Thames barges and possibly land them in compensation difficulties. Latton lock was shortened by 20 ft by building a masonry arch across the upper end of the chamber and rehanging the gates in 1837 as a test, the remainder being dealt with in 1841–2. The saving of water resulting from this shortening was some 20 per cent; unfortunately the locks (12½ ft) were not wide enough to pass two narrow boats at a time so the wastage was still considerable.

The year 1835 saw the resignation of William Hallett the first Chairman of the Company. He declined reelection as Chairman after 34 years and suggested the names of four local people as his successor, of these Ambrose Goddard, Lord of the Manor of Swindon was elected.[3]

In 1836 the GWR proposed in their third Bill realigning the canal in the Shrivenham area to save building six bridges and to ease their gradients and curves, Brunel producing a map of these changes.[14] The W&B were quick to notice that the plan cut off the Longcot branch and did not propose its restitution. As it was handling some 3,000 tons of coal each year this was a serious threat. Representations were made to Brunel as reported in a pathetic letter from W. Morse Crowdy to William Crowdy on 10th February, 1837.

We met Brunel and Saunders this day but I am sorry to say without coming to any terms, we cannot convince them of the loss of trade which we insist will follow the destruction of the branch. In fact they dispute us claiming anything for this – we are to see them again together to try and agree. There is at present so wide a difference between us that I much fear we shall have to oppose them. They are an overbearing Company and evidently hold us and any opposition we can offer very cheap. I rather despair, I confess, from the disposition they manifested today of our making any satisfactory arrangement with them.[15]

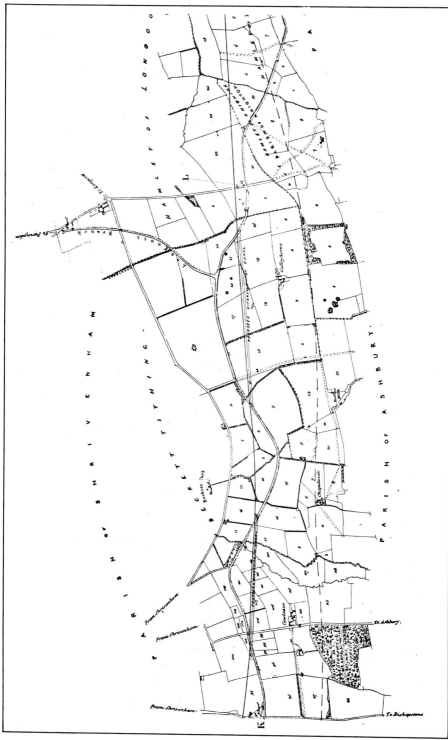

Brunel's diversion plan of 1836.

72

The W & B then issued a notice

> . . . no provision is made in this Bill to restore the branch on any other site and consequently that which they are proposing in term only to DIVERT and ALTER they do in fact mean to ABOLISH and DESTROY in direct violation of the 60th section of their original Act which expressly stipulates that they shall not divert the course of the Wilts and Berks unless with the consent of the Proprietors thereof.[16]

It is not known how the W & B achieved their aim of saving the Longcot branch, but an examination of the present line of the GWR shows it to run south of Brunel's line crossing the canal just once while the abandoned canal still snakes its way below Shrivenham and the branch, so wisely legalised in 1835, remains untouched.

Still seeking water the W & B made an agreement with Ambrose Goddard in 1838 to pay him £8 per year compensation for depriving Dray Mill of its ancient mode of irrigation by diverting water into the canal. This payment and an earlier one of £12 for the use of land at Swindon Wharf were paid regularly up to 1845, but then for some unknown reason they were allowed to lapse with consequences to be seen later.

In 1839 an appeal was sent to all Proprietors asking for "Donations for a subscription to the retiring Secretary Mr Dunsford, who had served the Company for 20 years. On his appointment in 1817 he found it £20,000 in debt and paying no dividends, not only had he cleared the debt but in 1839 the Company was paying £1.10s.0d per share." This appeal seems to have been premature, in 1877 Henry Lyde Dunsford explained that he had been Manager of the canal since the death of his father in 1845 and prior to that time he had acted as assistant for ten years and upward.[17]

Some letters from the estate of George Butler of Faringdon deposited in the Berkshire Record Office throw doubts on whether the father's efforts were always concerned with the wellbeing of his charge. Butler, holder of 94 W & B shares, whose trade was centered on Uffington Wharf, dealt in stone for local roads and was the recipient of a number of letters from traders complaining of Dunsford's management. In February 1833 Thomas Vincent of Semington Wharf of the K & A stated that he has been refused permission to examine the Company's books and in April 1836 he wrote again complaining of the high charges levied by the Company. He said that Dunsford was too preoccupied with his own stone, coal, salt and slate trade and that it was unjust that he should have control of tonnage rates and arrange these to his own advantage. Vincent affirmed that the original brick Priddy's bridge at Vastern which was in excellent condition has been taken down and replaced by a masonry one called Clarendon bridge built with stone supplied by Dunsford. He suggested that Somerset coal traders pay tonnage on returning empty boats but Dunsford's carrying Staffordshire coal did not, nor did his stone boats to the Worcester and Birmingham canal pay full rates. He suspected that some of these boats were actually Dunsford's property, repaired at Company expense and cited Richard Hodgson of Pewsham Lock House, the Company carpenter as witness to this.

Thomas Short of Abingdon charged Dunsford with selling stone above its real value and with buying timber of poor quality for repairs. He suspected that both Hallett, the Chairman, and Crowdy, the chief clerk are implicated with Dunsford and that the Committee of Management have no control over him. He refers to "The monstrous monopoly of Messrs Dunsford and Company, unfair in principle and unjust in practice."

Butler then wrote to the K & A and in July 1836 received a reply from their Chairman confirming that Vincent had once been employed by them and that his evidence was trustworthy. The K & A books were always available for Shareholder's inspection.

A minute from the W & B Committee of 26th January, 1837 ordered that the clerk was to refuse any inspection of the share or minute books as it was the opinion of the meeting that a Proprietor is not warranted in calling for such an inspection. What occurred over the next two years is not known but the Committee changed their minds and at their meeting of 4th April, 1839 Dunsford was ordered to meet Butler the following day, confirming that the books would be available to him. The outcome of the inspection is not recorded; it may be pure coincidence that Dunsford may have retired that year.

The deposited correspondence also contains a letter, dated 27th December, 1839 from Edward Leigh Bennet, a Lechlade clergyman, referring to the spring Committee meeting. Before 1838 summer freight had been refused owing to lack of water and for that reason tolls were kept as high as the Act allowed. They would probably have to be reduced later to combat railway competition. Proprietors could expect no further improvements in dividends excepting during an exceptionally rainy summer. A site for a new reservoir was available at Tockenham and this should be built as soon as possible to enable the materials for constructing the railway to be carried. It was expected that the increased carrying possible would pay for the reservoir which was built in 1839–40 having a surface area of 17 acres and by means of an open ditch and a culvert providing a supply at the head of Seven Locks at Trow Lane. The cost was £4,903.

References

1   Memoirs of W.M. Smith 1844 Phillips p81.
2   Grinsell & others, Studies in the history of Swindon.
3   BRO D EEL O & Bundle 1.
4   TS 207 20 12.
5   SRL Letter book 6th Dec., 1834.
6   SRL Letter book 9th June, 1826.
7   TS 207 27.
8   TS 167.
9   SRL Letter book 18th Oct., 1834.
10 TS 232 Nov 1834.
11 TS Siddington returns.
12 SRL Letter book 16th Jan., 1826.
13 Aris's Birmingham Gazette 8th July, 1833.
14 BRO QRUM 16.
15 WRO Accession 315.
16 TS 207 22.
17 SRL C171.

Chapter Eight
Letters and Coal

The W&B letter book preserved in Swindon Reference Library covers the period 7th August, 1824 to 18th March, 1839 and provides much information on the relationship between the W&B and neighbouring canals during that period. The letters, written by William Dunsford, the W&B Manager, illustrate how much of his time was taken up with the politics of running the canal trade, particularly with regard to coal.

The term "drawback" occurs many times, this being the name given to cash payments made to traders and carriers under certain conditions effectively reducing the tolls payable and thus enabling them to compete on more favourable terms with any opposition. For example the W&B attempted to compete in the Faringdon market against Forest of Dean coal unloaded at Radcot Wharf on the Thames by offering, together with the SCC and the Coal Owners, three shillings and sixpence for every ton of coal landed at Longcot and carted thence to Faringdon. Suppose the cost of coal at the pit plus the total tolls payable amounted to twenty-eight shillings and sixpence per ton, then such coal would cost the Trader twenty-five shillings. In this case the drawback would have been paid by the Longcot wharfinger to the trader on the production of a docket proving that the coal had passed through the Faringdon toll gate. Vincent, the trader involved, would not pass this reduction on to his customers so the offer was withdrawn. Dunsford writes that he regretted Vincent's action as he had hoped to make a considerable impression.

Such attempts to sell coal in areas normally served by other canals were common; at this time Strange, another W&B trader, was selling Somerset coal at Lechlade deep in T&S territory at twenty-six shillings and sixpence per ton.

In 1827 Vincent again aroused Dunsford's anger by making an agreement with the Oxford Canal Company,

> I hope you do not meditate the introduction of the Stafford coal at Wantage, as in that case I must candidly inform you that we expect a wharfage to be paid equivalent to the difference between it and the coal brought from Semington . . . I consider the importation of coal from the Oxford to our very best wharf as a most unfair use of our canal, and that we should combat such use with every weapon in our power. The Oxford canal will not suffer the Somerset coal to pass into their canal, and I cannot say I blame them. Of course they must expect equal obstruction as far as may be lawful.

There was a regular flow of letters between Dunsford and John Denyer the T&S Manager. When the NW was built the W&B hoped that the T&S would abandon the Thames except for local traffic; some years later Dunsford could not understand why Denyer seemed antagonistic to all his attempts to divert traffic to the W&B and away from the river,

> the time is gone for your large barges; even on the K&A they are getting into the 30 ton size. It therefore appears to me that your only hopes of a merchandise trade must be an amicable understanding with us, dismissing all jealousy of our interference with your seven miles between Latton and Inglesham and in fact regarding your canal as far as a through merchandise trade is concerned as terminating at our Junction.

In an attempt to divert from the Thames the trade in pig iron from Shropshire and elsewhere, and also to collect for both canals the traffic in manufactured iron from the mills along the western end of the T&S line which at this time was carried to London on the K&A, Dunsford suggested that both canals should charge two shillings and sixpence per ton tolls and wharfage on iron of every description passing through them. The W&B, whose line was the longer, were making a larger sacrifice in tolls, this he considered would offset the fact that the T&S was a wider canal and thus consuming more water per lock. Franklin, an Abingdon trader, was at this time very keen to carry such goods. Denyer refused to reduce the pig iron tonnage, claiming that to do so would be against T&S interests. Dunsford then asked "Why?" Denyer passed this letter to his Committee and Disney, the T&S Chairman, invited Dunsford to discuss the matter with that Committee at Latton. Dunsford then asked Denyer to prepare for him an account of the iron traffic between Brimscombe and Abingdon via the Thames since the opening of the NW and added a rebuke,

> My letters to you, I also wish to observe, were more of a private and confidential nature and with a view of ascertaining your sentiments previous to an official communication, than meant as direct official application to be scanned before the awful tribunal of a London board, which I shall beg to explain to the Gentlemen of your Committee when I have the pleasure of meeting them.

The proposed meeting did not take place, "Circumstances of a domestic nature" prevented Dunsford's attendance. The W&B Committee then directed him to attend a conference respecting toll rates on through trade as soon as this could be arranged.

Franklin persisted in seeking a reduction of tonnage from five shillings to two shillings and sixpence per ton for iron; Dunsford writes that the W&B are quite prepared to offer him such a reduction to promote new trade provided that the T&S do the same,

> It is in vain that they may expect to preserve any trade worth mentioning between Brimscombe and London – if such a delusion still persists it cannot last much longer. I have repeatedly offered to meet Mr Denyer in an equitable adjustment of the rates as will offer the trader a good living profit, which, if he have not, he cannot go on, and then what becomes of tonnage?

A similiar sentiment about the T&S reluctance to co-operate is contained in a letter to a Stroud brewer who had stated that the conveyance to Abingdon by the W&B was much more regular and safe than by the Thames. Dunsford writes

> Of this point no candid person can possibly entertain a doubt. The advantage has been obtained by an enormous outlay, at present unfortunately entirely profitless to the Proprietors. It is hoped that the reductions now made will induce you to continue your support to the canal which the Committee highly appreciate, but I am to add that the rates charged by the T&S cannot be admitted as an argument for the guidance of this Company in arranging theirs, as the anxiety of the Managers of that concern to cultivate the coal trade on the Wharves on the line of the Thames induces a disinclination to act in concern with us in points where a mutual good understanding would rebound to the advantage of both concerns.

The T&S did finally agree to reduce the tonnage on iron but the victory was apparently a hollow one for Franklin. Dunsford writes,

> In the course of the last summer your boats repeatedly passed our summit with lading so small as to afford us no remuneration for water and scarcely an average for wear and tear, yet in consideration of your exertions to promote trade we forbore to exercise our right of charging for 20 tons, while, if I am correctly informed the Thames and Severn charged you for 20 tons even when their water levels would not allow of your carrying half that quantity. The drawback they have at length granted on iron is a mere trifle compared to what their charges on your lading will be (averaging it at per ton) if this practice is continued.

When the NW was contemplated James Black, the T&S Engineer, had urged that a regulating lock with a one foot fall to Latton should be built; as already explained this was not done at the time. At a meeting of the T&S Proprietors on 3rd July, 1826 it was noted that on a number of occasions boats had passed from the NW when its water was lower by boatmen forcibly opening the T&S stop gate, and also that the W&B had refused admission to the NW when its level was higher.[1] Soon afterwards Dunsford writes to Denyer,

> I availed myself of the opportunity afforded by the recent evacuation of the Latton basin to fit the outer stop gate thoroughly in order that no infringement might take place of the clause in the Act which guaranteed the safety of your water. I am now preparing to put in another stop gate a boat's length from the present inner one in order to protect the water in our lower pound at such time as it happens to be higher than in your Latton pound. The waste on passing boats (when this work is effected) will be inconsiderable but in the present state of things (although I am happy to say we have enough water to last us through the dry season with care) I cannot reconcile it to any principle or justice to draw off 6 or 8 inches from a three mile pound on the passage of every boat to and from your canal.

This regulating lock was built on the flood aqueduct and communication between the two canals was reopened on 23rd June, 1826.

As a result of the July T&S meeting a letter was sent to the W&B Chairman by the T&S Chairman, Thomas Perry, who had taken over this post when John Disney had retired on 22nd April. In this Perry pointed out that the W&B had no right to announce to traders, as their notice of 6th June had done, that communication between the two canals would be stopped when the T&S water level was below that of the W&B, nor were the T&S bound to keep their level higher than was necessary for their own trade merely to prevent a loss of water by the W&B. He also reminded Hallett that

> Some very unjustifiable proceedings had taken place relating to the forcible opening of the protecting stop gate belonging to the T&S at Latton.

Dunsford was quite unperturbed by the arguments raging over his head, he writes to Denyer,

> To obviate further squabbles I have put up a regulating lock between us, I am now anxious to get your gate well fitted, that, when your pound is highest, there may be no water surreptitiously obtained from you. If you can lend us your stop planks for this purpose I shall be obliged to you.

In his letter of resignation to the T&S Proprietors John Disney stated,

> You now have a communication by water to Abingdon running parallel with the worst part of the Thames which keeps that uncertain navigation in check and has produced actual improvements on it."[1]

In a letter to the Hon. P.P. Bouverie, Lord Radnor's agent, Dunsford makes the first reference to the Gloucester–London fly boat trade, and almost incidentally opens up a correspondence which clears up a mystery,

> Messrs Franklin and Parker have recently been trying the experiment of working the small canal boat throughout and hitherto they have been successful. We find the trade with the Gloucestershire clothing districts increasing in consequence. In paying some land accounts in the year 1820 I found in our plan book the following memorandum "Lord Radnor was paid for 2 acres 1 rood 27 perches of land west of Acorn bridge, £165.5s.3d, this included the ground covered, which afterwards, the spoil bank being boated away, cleared the ground first covered by spoil bank, from hence it appears that the Company have paid for 1 acre and 16 perches which they have not taken, £77.0s.02d. I cannot discover at what period the spoil bank was carried away.

He then asks for settlement of the revised amount of £70.18s.9d. He had great difficulty in persuading F.J. Kelsey, Lord Radnor's steward that this land had never been conveyed to the Company and that by its not being fenced off his Lordship's tenant had the occupation of it for 20 years. The Company was prepared to waive any claim for rent over this period and merely wanted back the surplus paid by them for land which had never been theirs. To obtain the history of this plot he wrote to Priestley, his predecessor, reminding him that the note in the Plan book was in his writing. Priestley replied from Wakefield,

> There was at one time an intention of making a canal from the T&S to near the aqueduct, or between the aqueduct and the land in question, which if put into execution would have brought the land into wharfinger.

The mystery was solved, the land had obviously been earmarked when Black had proposed in 1797 joining the T&S with the W&B at this point. The land, now of course useless to the Company, was conveyed to them – obviously Lord Radnor did not want it either! This note of Priestleys can still be seen in the Plan book in Swindon Reference Library.

In mid 1827 the SCC and the coal owners suddenly withdrew their drawbacks. Dunsford writes to R. Savage at the SCC office at Bath,

> In the last six months 1,267 less tons of coal have been sold on our line and 576 less at Abingdon due to cuts in the price of Staffordshire coal. Since the SCC and the Owners have removed their drawback (two shillings per ton) dealers on the Thames cannot sell Somerset coal for less than thirty shillings per ton. Staffs coal sells at twenty-eight shillings and four pence being a reduction of five shillings due to the depressed state of the iron trade reducing the price at the pits. Something must be done to regain trade, but the W&B are not prepared to sacrifice more than their drawback of one shilling and sixpence per ton.

He was invited to attend a meeting of the SCC Committee but gained little satisfaction. On 24th October the W&B issued a notice removing their drawback on all coal, charging the full toll of six shillings and sixpence from Semington to Abingdon and five shillings and three pence from Latton; this produced the desired result for on 5th January, 1828 another circular was issued reducing the net toll from the K&A to Abingdon to three shillings and sixpence per ton. But all was not sunshine, the K&A then resolved to make a charge on empty boats passing through Bradford-on-Avon lock on their way back to the pits from the W&B, this had been waived up to this time by a gentleman's agreement. This charge would amount to an average increase in toll on laden boats of about 8d per ton and was probably introduced as a compensation for the drawbacks the K&A were offering to increase their Somerset coal trade northwards on the Thames from Reading.

Frustrated by the high price of Somerset coal Dunsford then turned his attention to providing alternative supplies from the Forest of Dean and Staffordshire. During the period 1785 to 1800 the T&S had imported large quantities of the latter but the route then available to them involved tranship-ment from narrow boats to Severn Trows at Stourport and again at Brims-combe from Trows to Thames Barges. Dunsford proposed using the same narrow boats all the way via the Birmingham and Worcester, the Severn, the Gloucester and Berkeley, Stroudwater and T&S. He writes to Denyer,

> As a certain quantity of Staffs coal will always be consumed at Abingdon our Committee are very desirous that some effort should be made to bring a portion of it through the T&S and NW. I presume that your tonnage is the same as upon Forest coal, and your drawback on entering our line the same as on the most favoured sort of the latter, but of this I should be glad to be informed previous to any attempt at an arrangement.

He then asks if any of the Forest traders had considered trying to break into the markets west of Swindon, i.e. Chippenham, Calne, Melksham etc. offering them every encouragement but warning Denyer that only the best Forest coal must be offered, inferior quality had done much previously in turning the public against it. He asked Denyer to consider this letter non-official and confidential.

Denyer's reply was evasive and once against he was asked to confirm that the rate for Staffs coal would be the same as for Forest, one shilling and sixpence; Dunsford reminding him that as boats would be travelling directly to and from the pits no wharfage would be payable. As many T&S Prop-rietors had investments in the Forest and few at this time had any connection with Staffs interests it is not surprising that Denyer was not at all helpful to the W&B over this scheme.

Despite Denyer's insistence that the toll would be two shillings Dunsford continued to plead for a one shilling reduction stating that only by such a concession could the W&B compete at Abingdon with Staffs coal carried by the Oxford canal and sold there at twenty-three shillings to twenty-five shillings per ton. Wharf room for storage would be made available so that the T&S need only be used when they had plenty of water to carry full cargoes.

> The Oxford Company are at present sending 18,000 tons of their coal per annum beyond Abingdon and I have long thought that having another line, practicable for a great part of the year for the same trade, we have been remiss in not endeavouring to obtain a slice of it.

He then approached Vincent of Abingdon to see if he would undertake to deliver Staffs coal to Wantage at a competitive price. Vincent had already been granted space at Wantage to store 500 tons. The proposed route was the old Birmingham canal, 10 miles, Birmingham to Worcester 30, Gloucester to Berkeley 8, Stroudwater 7, T&S 20, W&B 27, a total of 132 miles against the Oxford's 157, the total tolls being ten shillings and nine pence per ton. Vincent replied that he might be interested and asked for further details. He was told that he could land coal anywhere along the line and was warned of the possible dangers to boatmen experiencing Severn conditions for the first time and possible difficulties with water on the T&S. The largest boats should be used and stocks built up. Only the best coal should be bought, this stacks well and does not deteriorate.

> I am sanguine that these initiatory difficulties will yield to enterprise and perserverance, and the time is not far distant when the extraordinary anomaly of coal brought upwards of 130 miles being sold nearly 20 per cent cheaper than that brought 42 miles only will produce a change in the system of the Somersetshire Coal Masters and SCC alike beneficial alike to the Trader and the Public.

Dunsford also approached Franklin but his price

> Cannot be accepted as it is within a trifle of that at which the coal must sold at Abingdon (twenty-three shillings) – you may perhaps have calculated the T&S tolls at two shillings whereas they are only one shilling and sixpence.

Did Dunsford really expect the T&S to reduce their toll or was this a deliberate attempt to mislead Franklin? Vincent undertook at least one trip to the Staffs pits, he reports that his boatmen were not impressed either by the Severn or the T&S. A third Abingdon Trader was advised to lay in stocks of Staffs coal while T&S levels allow 25–26 ton loads, such coal should sell at 23 to 24 shillings per ton.

The reaction of the Oxford Company to this scheming was swift and dramatic. Dunsford writes to John Hodgkinson at the Navigation office, Birmingham,

> The few boats that have brought Staffs coal have excited the jealousy of the Oxford to an extraordinary degree, after several meetings of their committee they have determined to take the trade at Abingdon into their own hands, and their wharfinger has orders to watch our price and always to undersell us. Their large toll of seven shillings and five pence per ton gives them great latitude for this kind of opposition, and I have reason to believe that they would sacrifice half, or perhaps even two thirds, rather than have their Thames trade interfered with.

He then asks,

> Whether the owners of collieries not interested in the supply of the Thames trade through the Oxford would be induced to give a bonus if we dealt with them exclusively.

Later he visited Hodgkinson to discuss the coal trade and to ascertain whether stone could be carried back to Birmingham by the returning, otherwise empty, boats. He reported this visit to Denyer explaining that the back carriage of stone would only be feasible if the T&S would reduce their toll on this to one shilling per ton, the Worcester and Birmingham would charge ½d per ton mile. The T&S agreed to make this reduction on condition that at least 1,500 tons of coal or salt per annum passed down the NW.

Dunsford later wrote to Hodgkinson reporting continued opposition from the Oxford; he enclosed a hand bill of theirs which left a blank space for their price which they stated would always be 1d less per cwt than that charged by the W&B. The maximum price the W&B could charge at Abingdon was twenty-five shillings, it cost them twenty-four shillings to get it there and a further two shillings for storage etc. So every ton lost one shilling and as each ton displaced coal which could be sold at a profit of three to four shillings there was little sense in carrying on were it not a means of fighting encroachment by the Oxford into W & B markets. That Company offered a drawback of four shillings a ton to Wantage, a public wharf and secretly paid most of the wharfage. He suggests that the loss be shared by the Worcester and Birmingham allowing a further drawback of 6d per ton on coal bound for the W & B. He asked whether Birmingham architects could be persuaded to use stone for facings instead of the newly developed concrete.

In a later letter to Denyer Dunsford encloses accounts of all trade between their canals, emphasising the decline in Forest trade and suggesting that Staffs coal could restore his loss in tolls if he would only encourage it. Back carriage of goods to Birmingham would also effectively reduce the price of Staffs coal, Hallett suggesting that the W & B exercise their right to charge empty boats would encourage traders to seek back cargoes. Dunsford offered to carry grain for Parker of Whitney for three shillings per quarter.

The final blow to Dunsford's hopes was struck by the T & S charging two shillings and sixpence per ton on three cargoes of Staffs coal. He writes a bitter letter to Denyer

– but if you persist in charging the full two shillings and sixpence I shall give up. For the sake of general encouragement we are willing to submit to the comparative loss at Swindon, Wootton Bassett, Uffington and Longcot as between your coal and Somerset. Surely it is obvious that you should not stand niggling (excuse the phrase) whether your coal goes a few miles more or less but let it all come at one shilling and sixpence. Somerset is to you (as compared to our line) what Stafford is to us at Abingdon and Wantage. In fact our interest in selling Staffs coal is loss but for the hope of back carriage.

Denyer was unmoved and Dunsford expresses his regret in two letters,

I perused your letter with the greatest concern as the intimation it conveys is a complete extinguisher of the trade in Staffs coal east and west of here.

I trust I may be permitted to express my regret that the experiment of the Staffs coal trade has not been allowed a trial. Although from this point I shall cease to take an active part in pushing the Staffs coal, I will not discourage it.

One last exchange of letters took place on this subject, Dunsford writes to Denyer,

. . . in the course of the last year (1829) we pushed the trade in Staffs coal from Wantage into the K & A district in south Berkshire, this trade could be increased but not at a profit. If I send a boat of this coal via Semington and the K & A to Hungerford you charge two shillings, but if I take it to Wantage you charge 6d more. . . . I have so often urged it as a matter of policy in your Company to reduce your toll to one shilling and sixpence that I fear you will be wearied by the repetition of the Cuckoo note, but I might ask you what you have done by your recent advance and by keeping your full tolls to here, Uffington and Wantage? But so odd is your policy that where there is most need of reduction your tolls are highest. I mentioned to Mr Palmer and Mr Salt that if your placed Wantage on the same footing as Abingdon I would lay in 500 tons of Staffs coal as soon as possible. I hope you will ultimately see it in your interest to do still more.

Denyer's reply was that the T & S was being asked to sacrifice half their toll while the W & B were only to give up one quarter, whereupon Dunsford proceeded to give him a lesson in arithmetic and continued,

> We are all liable to errors and these little slips as to figures may well be overlooked among friends – but when you proceed further to reason offensibly upon your own erroneous premises, more than hinting that you suspect some unfair design on our part, I begin to suspect that you are not "the very King of Courtesy" . . . I beg the favour of your communicating to me what you consider a fair proportion on each side, I am sanguine that we shall not differ much.

He then wrote to Mr Palmer making concrete proposals to be laid before their next Committee meeting. Palmer invited him to that meeting but once again Dunsford made the excuse that he could not attend. As if deliberately to antagonise the T&S he stated that, while not wishing to make threats, the salt merchant at Wantage could more easily, and at greater profit to the W&B get his salt via the Oxford, and that as he was to supply stone to a new church at Coventry he would have 70 to 80 boats on that canal in the coming summer he could easily bring coal back to Wantage that way.

When the T&S had frustrated Dunsford's efforts to set up a trade in Staffs coal he turned his attention to carrying on the war with the Oxford by making a general proposal for establishing a trade in Somerset coal at Oxford. A suitable agent would be S.W. Hopkins whose base was at Friar's Wharf, he having ample storage space and no connection with the Oxford Canal Company. The coal owners and W&B would be stockholders without the possibility of loss. The agent, in consideration of no capital being expected of him, would make every effort to sell as much as possible at a moderate commission. Durnford hoped to sell 3–4,000 tons a year at twenty-five shillings per ton, the rival OCC price being twenty-eight shillings and four pence. He then put this proposal to the SCC asking whether coal could be produced at the pits for ten shillings to assist the project, the W&B being willing to charge only two shillings for their 52 miles. There is no recorded reply to this offer but we will see in a later letter that a trade to Oxford was started on a small scale at this time.

Staffordshire coal sales at Abingdon continued to worry the OCC whose agent, Mr Copland, stated in a letter dated 13th April, 1830

> Sold over 1,400 tons of coal, severe competition from Staffs coal arriving via the Wilts and Berks canal."[2]

Dunsford now attempts to break the Somerset coal owners monopoly. He writes to Elijah Bush of Trowbridge,

> Having accidently heard that you are concerned in a coal works at Radstock which does not recognise the combination so long established by the other Somersetshire Coal Owners to the great inconvenience of the Trade and injury to the Public at large, I am induced to trouble you with an enquiry as to the terms on which throughout the winter you would furnish me with 3 to 6 boat loads per week, and in the event of your coal suiting the Berkshire market it would be in my power to give it a decided preference at Wantage and Abingdon. And I beg to assure you that I feel every disposition to do so. Be good enough to favour me with a reference to whom I should apply.

Bush passed this letter to Blacker, Collins and Co, Tyning Coal Works, Radstock whose reply and quoted price was not what Dunsford had hoped.

He writes

> I was duly favoured with your letter by which it appears that your prices are the same as your neighbours. I can have no objection to trying your coal in common with that of the other works, and I have no doubt but that it is, as you say, fully equal to any on the market. But this is not exactly what I meant by applying to Mr Bush. Having been given to understand that you were unfettered by any obligations to sell at a stipulated price or to give a stipulated weight, or to raise only a stipulated quantity, . . . I thought that you might be induced by the advantage I held out of giving you almost a monopoly of the trade at Wantage and Abingdon (provided always that your coal would suit the market) to give me a commensurate advantage . . . such as allowing a certain sum per ton by way of discount on being paid for every 500 tons. I trust that the assumption that you do not belong to the banded combination of the other coal owners means that there is nothing preposterous in my entertaining such an expectation. If your sale by land is so brisk as to enable you to dispose of all your working, of course such a proposal as mine holds forth no temptation, but if you are willing and able to increase your quantity, the opportunity presents itself, in the shape I have stated, or by any other means you may deem more eligible . . . This is the point for you to determine, but at any rate I trust you will feel no offence at the proposition but consider it a *bona fide* made in the fair spirit of Trade. My object being to increase the Sale rather than the retail profit, . . . I intend, should you do anything worth notice in the way of reduction, to give the Public the full benefit of it, being quite contented with the profit as it now stands, but not at all with the price or quantity sold.

It is not known what reduction, if any, was offered, but two months later Dunsford wrote again to Blacker Collins & Co specifying the type of coal required at Wantage and continues,

> I intend to keep a pair of boats regularly on, which will generally make the trip in the course of the week.

The letter book contains a report of a Committee meeting on 9th September, 1831.

> Since the opening of the Gloucester and Berkeley canal, the trade which subsisted between Bristol and Oxford through the K&A and this canal has been gradually declining both as to corn and general merchandise, and more especially the transit of Irish oats has been entirely diverted to the port of Gloucester, and thence by the Stroud, T&S and the Thames to Oxford. Ordered that the Superintendent do represent these circumstances to the Agent of the K&A for the purpose of submitting to their Committee the expediency of reducing the tolls throughout their lines and on the Avon River by at least one half on corn and one third on merchandise with a view to the recovery of the said trade.

Dunsford writes a series of letters to J.S. Moline of the K&A first seeking and then acknowledging the asked for reduction in grain tolls; the K&A would not, however, allow any relaxation in Somerset coal tonnage. Dunsford agrees to a drawback on boats trading to Bristol with stone and returning with coal from the Avon railway, but bewails the fact that not only does the K&A refuse to abandon their charge on empty boats returning from Wantage and beyond but also intend to charge on those returning from the Avon, these had previously passed without toll.

The carriage of coal to Oxford had continued since 1829 on a small scale; in March 1833 the K&A reduced their toll on this traffic. Five years later they were considering abolishing all drawbacks. Dunsford, writing to C. Brand recounts how drawbacks had increased the Oxford trade in Somerset coal from 300 tons in 1832–3, to 900 in 1835–5, 1,289 in 1836 and 1,416 in 1837. Greater increases were not possible as the coal was now two shillings and sixpence dearer at the pits, and because only one trader, Mr Hopkins, was involved, the others were afraid of offending the OCC. He asks if a further reduction is possible, and continues,

> If the K&A abolish their drawback the W&B, and I presume the Coal Canal Lock Fund will do likewise and the trade will be lost.

The reply came from S. Robbins of Honeystreet Wharf, and in answer Dunsford writes,

> I regret that the K&A consider the amount of tonnage to the W&B so small that they cannot afford any reductions, it is £3,000 per annum, hardly small, and it certainly will not be increased by abolishing drawbacks. You appear to consider drawbacks in the light of a mere "douceur" or bonus to the Traders which may as well be saved by the Company, I on the contrary deem them as a means of inviting trade which would not exist without them. Take the Oxford trade, the full Parliamentary rates on all canals is ten shillings and eight pence per ton, drawbacks reduce this to four shillings and four pence. To meet competition the coal must be sold at twenty-five shillings per ton. I admit that it is a small trade, but it is a growing one, and the Gas Company are using more and more Somerset rubble, an extra one shilling per ton would turn the scale. In conclusion I beg to observe that the drawback system has worked well in this concern and I feel that judicious allowances are the means of promoting trade, and that instead of saying you cannot afford to yield up a portion of your Parliamentary rates (which are too high anyway) you should rather say you cannot afford to charge them – not forgetting the homely adage that half, nay even a quarter of a loaf is better than no bread.

Finally a letter on petty theft, the bane of all canal Companies,

> To J. Theobalds, Semington, 3rd November, 1824.
>
> On the 28th of last month a boat belonging to D. Powell of Shrivenham and steered by a man named Fowler arrived at Marston lock and attempted to pass without a permit, but was prevented by Mr Reeve who very properly detained the boat till the tonnage was paid for the cargo she then on board, coal 22 tons 15 cwt. As Powell has not been in the habit of bringing such small cargoes, there is reason to suppose that some of the coal must have been sold on the road, and thus the Company has been defrauded of this tonnage. As you are too well acquainted with your duty as Collector not to have sent forward to Melksham or Pewsham locks to have this boat stopped supposing as I do that she must have passed your lock surreptitiously I must conclude that there has been some neglect or connivance somewhere. I must therefore desire you to acquaint me with every particular within your knowledge relative to this flagrant violation of the rules that the parties who are guilty may be punished as they deserve and that the owner and steerer may be dealt with according to the Law.
>
> Waiting your answer,
> I am
> Yours, William Dunsford.

References

1 TS 166.
2 Oxford Canal Co. records OXC/88/1.

Chapter Nine
The Years of Decline, 1841–1877

The GWR line from London to Bristol was opened on 30th June, 1841, and running as it did almost alongside the W&B all the way from Abingdon through Swindon to Chippenham, rapidly took over almost all the local traffic. The coal route from the Somerset pits was not duplicated so the coal trade was not immediately affected. The Swindon to Abingdon section suffered most; here the railway built stations wherever the canal had wharves except at Wantage where the line ran some two miles to the north, and Abingdon, whose citizens had refused to grant the railway passage.

A study of the trade figures given in Appendix 5 and those of the number of boats crossing the summit (Appendix 6) illustrate this decline. In connection with the latter figures it should be noted that throughout the life of the canal four fifths of the trade moved from west to east, the boats returning empty.

In June 1843 the Canal Company made an agreement with the GWR to allow them to take water from the summit level for their houses and works at Swindon and for condensing steam, this latter to be returned to the canal. The GWR were to make the necessary constructions including a measure of the quantity of water taken; if they obstructed the canal a fine of £50 per day would be imposed. They could not take more than 60,000 cubic feet per week, this to be taken between noon on Saturday and noon on Sunday. £50 was charged every three months plus a further £1 for every 12,775 cu. ft taken over and above an annual 2,225,000 cu. ft. They built two reservoirs and a short feeder from the NW, but shortly after only one was in use. From June 1844 to July 1867 they paid, apart from the £200 fixed charge, an extra £190 rising finally to £640 per annum.

The impact of the GWR on Swindon was enormous. The locomotive works was in full use by early 1843 and the Company provided for the welfare of their workpeople in a new town which grew up independent of Old Swindon. In 1831 the population of Old and New Swindon was 1,742, by 1851 it was 4,876 and by 1871 11,720. But while the population was increasing it brought no increase in revenue to the W&B. Martin Smith has made a study of the Swindon Wharf trading accounts and extracted the following statistics.[1]

Year	Exports in tons	Imports in tons	Total tolls
1818–20	260	2,479	£434
1844–5	860	4,486	£712
1857–8	686	5,238	£337

It can be seen that the difficulties the Company found itself in lay not so much in decreasing trade but in the decreasing income from tolls, reductions in these being forced upon them by railway competition. In 1857 coal from Semington to Swindon was charged one shilling and sixpence per ton, £2.0s.6d for 27 tons instead of the £4.11s.1d payable in 1844, and that from Abingdon two shillings per ton. Iron ore from Semington was down to one shilling per ton. Stone, bricks and tiles were charged ½d per ton mile instead of the 1½d of 1844. In 1857–8 no goods left Swindon on the NW (102 tons

1844–5) while only 63 tons stone, 86 tons gravel and 65 tons of salt were imported via Latton. Receipts from Abingdon trade were only £4.7s.1d (including 30 tons Midland coal) in 1857–8 compared with £28.16s.11d (185 tons coal) in 1844–5. Only 24 tons of stone left Swindon.

By 1844 the NW salt trade had almost all been transferred to rail as also had part of the coal trade. Swindon imported 1,200 tons less by canal in 1857–8 compared with 1844–5 despite the fact that the population had risen to 6,200. By 1857 no Forest or Staffs coal arrived at Swindon Wharf, the rail links to Gloucester and Oxford had killed this trade. The opening of the Cheltenham and Great Western Union railway to Kemble in 1841 and to Gloucester in 1845 seriously reduced NW trade which fell from 783 tons in 1837 to only 445 in 1844. A further blow fell when the Wilts, Somerset and Weymouth railway was opened in 1848 from Chippenham via Melksham to Westbury, the branch to Frome allowed Radstock coal to be exported to Westbury and beyond, reducing the quantity available to the SCC.

In 1852 the K&A, similarly in difficulties, was taken over by the GWR. The Act contained a clause agreeing that the W&B traffic would pay less than the maximum toll on their essential Semington to Dundas link as long as they allowed traders a similiar concession.[2] The W&B also approached the GWR offering a similar transfer but the Railway, having nothing to fear from them, proposed a purchase price of £20,000 which the Company, unwisely it turned out later, refused.[3]

The number of boats passing east of Swindon had fallen from 2,674 in 1837 to 964 in 1864, those passing west from 2,475 to 1,289, while the number in and out of the NW had fallen from 793 to 332. The total tonnage handled was 56,266 of which Somerset coal was still the greatest part. More coal was carried to wharves west of Swindon (25,046 tons in 1862 compared with 18,419 in 1837), but to Swindon itself and wharves to the east, the tonnage had fallen to 10,690 compared to 23,482 largely due to the loss of trade in Abingdon and from there up and down the Thames. Of all the wharves east only Stratton and Wantage showed increases. The trade in other commodities did not decrease so much, 23,109 tons in 1837 to 18,374 in 1863, the loss being chiefly due to the decline in corn growing, the ratio of pasture to arable land increasing because of the repeal of the corn laws in 1846.

In 1863 the Somerset and Dorset Railway purchased and closed the tramway from Radstock to Midford on the SCC; coal supplies, the bread and butter trade of the W&B, were further reduced. This, combined with the inability to finance proper maintenance caused trade to deteriorate even more rapidly. By 1870 the total tonnage had fallen to 34,879 (20,595 coal) and in 1876 to 27,431 (12,461 coal). The Company had made economies in staff, those remaining had their salaries steadily reduced over the years. The post of wharfinger was abolished at Swindon in 1861 and at Abingdon in 1867. These economies resulted in poorer maintenance, traffic delays, and the lack of personal promotion of trade, all of which helped to depress trade even more. In 1835 John Theobalds, the toll collector at Semington, was earning £70 per annum, in 1850 this was reduced to £54.12s.0d and in 1851 to £46.16s.0d. He died in 1867 being replaced by R. Batt from the Bath office, then closed. Like Theobalds he served the Company for at least 57 years.

In 1866, for reasons not apparent till later, the GWR were given notice that they must stop taking water from the canal and remove all their equipment from canal land by 7th July, 1867.[4]

The W & B paid a final dividend of £561 in 1871; there was a small sum for disposal in 1872 but this was retained pending the outcome of litigation with the Swindon Waterworks Company (founded 1866). The canal Company claimed that the latter was diverting Wroughton Brook into their reservoir to the detriment of W & B supplies. The case was heard before Vice-Chancellor Malins on 3rd December, 1873 and the canal Company fared badly. In evidence H.C. Crowdy admitted that for 34 years no annual general meeting of the Proprietors had been called either by circular or advertisement and that at a meeting arranged on 1st July, 1870 to file this suit he was the only Proprietor present. He took the chair and transacted, by himself, the whole of the business.

The judgement was that the Company had no exclusive right to the waters they claimed and even if they had, the abstraction by the waterworks was not such an amount as would justify any complaint. It was clearly established that, except temporarily during the exceptionally dry year of 1870, there had not been, nor was there now any deficiency of water. The canal Company only had a right to water for use in the canal and had no right to interfere with the proper, useful and beneficial use of water in the district for the support of human life. To emphasise that there was plenty of water it was pointed out that for many years the Company had been selling, illegally, over 100,000 gallons per day to the railway. Finally, they were reminded that the NW Act specified that the NW should not take any water from Thames sources. Wroughton Brook was a Thames tributary so its water could not legally be used by the NW as it had been for many years thanks to the connection by the canal main line.[5]

In 1873 a meeting was held at Wantage to consider the building of a tramway to link the town with the GWR. Mr Ormond, a solicitor, was the principal proponent and reported that an application had been made to the W & B for permission to place a bridge across the canal. They were willing to allow this but imposed a penalty of £100. This Ormond considered obstruction and he stated that if this was the way the canal Company proposed to deal with the matter, the sooner they died out the better, and as one of the shareholders he did not care how soon as the canal was little better than a muddy ditch.[6] That "muddy ditch" still managed to carry nearly 2,000 of coal to Wantage that year. The charge was nothing out of the ordinary; in 1872 the GWR was charged £100 for the right to widen their bridge over the NW in Swindon, and furthermore had to agree to light the towpath under the bridge for evermore. In 1877 James Hinton paid £200 for the right to build Cambria bridge over the main line in Swindon.

The Wantage Tramway was built, its largest engineering work being a girder bridge with a 38 ft span over the W & B main line at Grove. By 1878 the tramway had bought an engine, No 5, the famous *Jane* which was capable of hauling goods wagons. The emphasis turned away from Somerset and Gloucester coal, in the early 1880s the tramway imported coal from Cannock Chase, the Forest of Dean and Moira seling at eighteen to twenty-two shillings per ton.

Ormond of Wantage, although holding 84¼ shares, was no supporter of the W&B Company; in July 1874 he was spokesman of a group of influential shareholders who pressed the Company, demanding its closing down.

> The K&A, belonging as it does to the GWR, would hardly oppose such closing, neither would the T&S. The question is whether it is competent for the Company to cease to take tolls, to cease to maintain the waterway, the bridges, locks, wharves and roads connected with it, in fact to abandon the use of the canal entirely and to discharge their servants and other officers leaving the Public and especially the Traders, Landowners and other persons possessing rights or easements in connection with the canal to use and enjoy them as best they may.

The Company could not ignore this group holding 450 shares so they wrote to Counsel, one W.T. Friend, seeking advice.

> The GWR by extension of their branches to Abingdon, Wantage and Calne have further damaged the interests and traffic of the Company and it has yearly become more evident by the diminished receipts that ultimately the greater portion, if not all the carrying trade of the District will be accomplished by the railway. Under the circumstances it has become a very grave question with the Management of the Canal Company whether the time has not come for them to adopt measures for winding up the Company whilst it is still in the position to show a small profit, rather than to wait until the absorption of the business by the railway shall reduce the Company to a state of insolvency.

Friend replied,

> Only an Act of Parliament could close the canal and realise its assets, this would not be forthcoming as long as any profit whatever can be derived, that is as long as the tolls collected exceed the cost of their collection and the absolutely necessary outlay for keeping the canal in useable order. I do not think that the circumstances of the undertaking being a profitless one to the present Company, having regard to the capital they have expended, is a sufficient motive for inducing the Legislature to pass an Act which would be destructive to the rights of the Public and of the parties having particular rights and interests. Such an Act would amount to special legislature in favour of one only of the several parties to the original statutory bargain made between the Company, the Public and the Landowners for no other reason than that such bargain has in event turned out to be a bad one for the party seeking to be relieved of it. The existing Acts define the conditions on which the Company can obtain relief and be able to realise their remaining property, the canal must have been disused for a period of 14 years. Finally, either one or other of two propositions must be clear, either tolls are worth collecting or they are not. If they are, there is no good reason for Parliament closing the canal as the Company's course is clear, they must either sell to a Company with smaller capital whose proportionate profit will be larger, and seek an Act to do so, or to increase tolls – or maybe even lower them to encourage trade. The alternative is to wait until it is only a loss to collect the tolls, and then by discontinuing to take them, commence the period of 14 years of "discontinuance and disuse" contemplated by the Act, and when this period has run for some time, apply to Parliament for its abridgement on the grounds of the effect of the unanticipated development of railways, and then sell the disused undertaking.

The Company were still uncertain whether if they ceased to take tolls they could get rid of the burden of maintenance so they sought more advice. This time the answer came from J.H. Lloyd in August 1874 who stated that if they took no tolls they could not be compelled to maintain, quoting as precedents the cases of the Wey and Arun Junction canal and the Bradford navigation. They now decided to take positive action.

The *North Wilts Herald* of 5th September reported the discussions about closure, the article stating that only one trader, Mr Hiskins of Wantage was active at that date. On the 21st November a long notice appeared in the same paper.

Wilts and Berks Canal.

Powers to sell and transfer the undertaking, or to close the canal for traffic and sell the site thereof, winding up and dissolution of the Company, compensation to Officers, amendment or repeal of Acts and other purposes.

Notice is given that application is to be made to Parliament for an Act for the above purpose. If the undertaking be not sold as a whole, to make provision for closing the canal for traffic, and for discontinuing the preserving, maintaining and using the canal locks, reservoirs and other works of the Company, to extinguish or provide for the extinguishing of all tolls, rates, duties, charges and all rights of any liberties.

The *Bristol Daily Post* of 23rd November reported that

The Bristol Chamber of Commerce, the Mayor and Merchants of Bristol protested at the Swindon meeting, their protests being rebuffed by the canal manager.

The *Wilts and Gloucester Standard* of 20th January, 1875 reported,

A meeting was held at Chippenham by landowners to discuss the proposed closure; they expressed concern about water supplies. J.C. Townsend stated that the Railway had the right to make a station at every wharf along the canal, and by owning the K & A and putting tolls on Somerset coal to a maximum they had made it impossible for the canal to compete. He said that the condition of the canal was bad, it had recently taken ten days to get a load to Wantage and three boats to do it, the depth of water being so little and the locks and bridges so out of repair. He suggested that Parliament should be approached by stating that whereas the canal Company had built the canal in good faith, Parliament, by allowing railways, had ruined it. There were rumours of a new Company being formed to run the canal.

A Bill was prepared late in 1875,

To authorise the Company of Proprietors of the Wilts and Berks Canal Navigation to sell and transfer their undertaking, or to provide for the closing of the Canal and the sale of the site thereof, and for other purposes. And whereas the traffic on the canal has of late decreased and the receipts are so reduced as to be insufficient to maintain the canal and to yield a profit to the Proprietors. The Company is to be wound up under the provisions of the Companies Acts 1862 and 1867. The Court of Chancery may sell by public auction or private contract the canal and all its Assets, the money so obtained to be disposed in accordance with Orders of Court. . . . If within one year of the passing of this Act no sale or transfer has been affected the canal shall be closed to traffic and all assets sold, the money to be the assets of the Company. If sold in lots the owner of land abutting on the canal shall be entitled to purchase up to the centre of the canal. When the Company are bound to maintain any bridges, fences or other work . . . after the closing of the canal, the Company shall out of any monies received make compensation to the owner of the land on which such works are constructed. The Company shall out of any monies they shall receive . . ., put in good and substantial repair any public bridges, roads or culverts which they were liable to repair or maintain previously to the passing of this Act. The Company shall pay to the Superintendent of the canal any sum they may think fit as compensation for any loss he may sustain by reason of the transfer or sale of the canal.

The prospectus issued sought a capital of £20,000 in 400 shares of £50 each and stated,

A general opinion has been expressed by practical men acquainted with the Wilts and Berks and other canals that if a moderate sum be expended in restoring the canal to an efficient state it will speedily and profitably obtain a large increase of the traffic in timber and other heavy articles at present conveyed by the railway, and further that by the establishment of agencies in the cities of Bristol, Bath and elsewhere business not hitherto sought after will be ensured.[7]

The threatened closure was averted by an agreement with a new Company who wished to purchase the concern and sought powers to close the Longcot branch and sell the site thereof. A study of the trade figures show that in 1870 only 35 tons had been discharged at Longcot, 58 in 1871, 34 in 1874 and none in 1875 and 1876.

The Act received the Royal Assent on 27th June, 1876 as *39–40 Vic. Cap. 59* but by this time had changed almost beyond recognition. The title was, "An Act for incorporating the Wilts and Berks Canal Company, for the transfer to the of the undertakings of the Wilts and Berks Canal Navigation and for other purposes." The preamble restates the reason for the transfer. The new Company consisted of George Frederick Fox, Samuel Jones, Robert Choules, Adam Twine, Thomas Turner, James Hiskins, Henry Taylor, Robert Pictor and Joseph Barnes. Of these, three were names which had at times appeared in the trading records. Adam Twine was recorded as being the lockeeper at Seven Locks from 1810 to 1815 and later as trading in coal and stone to Wootton Bassett. James Hiskins traded also in coal and stone to Wantage. James Barnes rented the house and wharf at Dauntsey and later the wharf at Hay Lane and the counting house at Swindon. George Frederick Fox was a Bristol solicitor.

The purchase price was £13,496.5s.0d to be paid within two months. All current rents, tolls, profits etc were to be apportioned between the old and new Companies by Henry Lyde Dunsford. Many sections of the earlier Acts were repealed. The canal was at all times to be kept open and navigable. Swindon New Town was given powers to erect bridges and Gas and Water Companies powers to lay mains across the canal. The capital of the new Company was to be £30,000. The personal estate of the Company was 511¼ shares purchased out of funds earlier, all books of accounts, maps etc and the furniture at Swindon, one steam dredger, iron cranes at Abingdon, Swindon, Laycock and Melksham, all boats and tools.[8]

In May 1876 the Wilts, Somerset and Berks Canal Traders Association, soon to become the new Company lodged a complaint with the Board of Trade that the GWR had acted "prejudicially to their interests by increasing tolls on canal traffic proportionally higher than those on rail". The 1873 Regulation of Railways Act had specified that the GWR rate for coal should be ½d per ton mile but this could be varied following two months notice.[2]

References

1   Martin Smith. Thesis SRL.   4   SRL E2.
2   PRO Kew MT6 176/9.   5   SRL E5, E6.
3   GWR Mss letter, W. Foote to Sir   6   Higgins *The Wantage Tramway*.
    Daniel Gooch.   7   Prospectus, Devizes Museum.
                                                 8   JHC Vol 131 14 Feb–27 June 1876.

Chapter Ten
Under New Owners, 1877–1914

The transfer to the new Company did not take place until 1877. At a meeting of the old Company at Swindon on 15th March that year Mr H.C. Crowdy, the chief clerk, reported that the conveyance was ready for completion and that the new Company had the balance of the purchase money. It was resolved that the remaining assets of the old Company be retained to meet liabilities and that notice of the transfer, of the winding up of the old Company and of the monetary distribution be published.

The new owners increased the capital to £30,000, the difference presumably being spent on improvements, but to no avail, tolls had fallen to £800 by 1882. Trade records were carried on in the old books under the heading "The New Company" but entries became rare. Taunt's *Illustrated Map of the Thames, 1878* reports "Hardly any traffic to Abingdon, but beyond Swindon to Semington it commands a fair amount of traffic in coal, timber &c."

On the 13th April, 1880 two Bristol solicitors, G.F. Fox and F.E. Whittuck lent the Company £400, half to be repaid in October 1880 and the remainder in April 1881 plus interest at 5 per cent per annum. By an Indenture of Mortgage dated 5th March, 1881 John Arscott of Plympton and Henry Tombs of Swindon paid the Company £3,975 for its surplus lands.

In 1882 the canal and its revenue was leased to an organisation of gentlemen in Bristol who were largely connected with Bristol docks, Charles Nash, a timber merchant, Mark Whitwell, a ship owner and John Dixon, a dock manager. They appointed H.G. Allen to manage the concern. By an Indenture of 18th July, 1882 the canal was granted for 21 years, the lease could be ended after 14 years. The yearly rental was £1,250 which enabled the 1876 Company to pay a dividend of 4 per cent. They retained the right of inspection and the new group or the Mortgagees could sell certain lands. Both Companies were to share equally the cost of opposition by the latter to the Calne Water works and to the T&S Bill which sought to turn that canal into a railway. Any disputes between the 1876 and 1882 groups were to be decided by two arbitrators.

The 1882 T&S Bill referred to was opposed by a coalition of the Stroudwater, Sharpness, W&B, the Severn Commissioners and the Staffs and Worcester, this coalition calling themselves "The Allied Navigations". The W&B were in no position to do much; in fact of the group only the Stroudwater and Staffs and Worcs were solvent. Their efforts did succeed in defeating the Bill, but instead of their gaining control as they hoped, the GWR stepped in to take over the T&S to prevent any further attempts to convert it into a railway.

The *Devizes and Wilts Gazette* of 27th April, 1897 tells how the new group did their utmost to foster and stimulate trade on the canal by putting as much as possible of their own traffic on it. They experimented with sectional boats "with approved stem and stern and body like a centipede which could be cut asunder, portions of the body about the length of a railway truck could be left or collected from wharves en route." But difficulties of steering and loading, and separation of the body "at inconvenient times" led to failure of the scheme and standard narrow boats were used again. The "freightliner" boats were also found to be most unsuitable for use on the Avon.

By 1888 the Bristol group had lost £16,000 and sought to give up their lease, to do this they paid a forfeiture sum of £1,000. By this time the Somerset coalfield was almost worked out, at least as far as the SCC was concerned. This carried only 24,500 tons in 1884 and 11,500 in 1893. Pumping to the summit ceased in 1898 and the canal was declared derelict in 1902. As coal became less and less available so the main reason for the existence of the W&B subsided with it.

In 1888 the W&B carried a total of 33,000 tons and collected £843 in tolls, this, together with an income from rents and the sale of water (£950) allowed £1,166 to be spent on maintenance. £50 to be paid as the Manager's salary and a dividend of £607 to be distributed. In the same year the GWR were again authorised to take water from the NW, this time by pipeline for which supply they paid £250 per annum, increasing to £300 in 1891.

The 1876 Company continued to work the canal until 1891 when another new group, the United Commercial Syndicate took over. They raised £4,489 for the Company by means of a Mortgage on Coate reservoir and the annual GWR water payments. Lord Wantage advanced £10,000 and also provided the £4,489, the Mortgage being transferred to him as security. They also raised money by 5 per cent debentures.

An observer remarked in 1889 that the canal east of Swindon appeared unused; it had a green film in places with patches of rushes and undisturbed flowers.

The Syndicate under their Manager W.J. Ainsworth spent about £16,000 on dredging and lock repairs, putting the canal in substantially efficient working order from Semington to Swindon. They formed a separate carrying organisation and operated a service of twelve regular fast boats but no new trade was created; by using their own boats they took the existing trade from the original boatmen who lost £840 in less than two years while the carrying concern lost £843. Tolls for 1891 – 3 averaged £600, this with the water sales produced a net balance of about £130.

By 1894 the canal had silted up to a depth of two feet; the maximum loading of boats was 18 tons instead of the 35 they were built to carry.

On 17th August, 1894 an Act (57–58 Vic. Cap. 194) "to confirm a provisional order made by the Board of Trade under the Railway and Canal Traffic Act 1888" became law. This lengthy Act, divided into three parts, empowered Railway and Canal Companies to modify their Parliamentary tolls. Special sections applied only to certain canals, that concerning the W&B allowed substantial increases, particularly in tolls on empty boats. The minimum toll for all boats passing through one or more locks was to be two shillings and sixpence per ton. For empty boats which had not carried cargo already charged at two shillings and sixpence per ton, or on its way to collect such cargo the toll was five shillings. Long lists were included covering every type of merchandise imaginable, these being classified into eight types paying different rates per ton mile and wharfage. Tolls varied according to the number of miles goods were carried, for example, classes A & B 0.6d per ton mile for the first 10 miles, 0.5d for the next, 0.4 the next 10 and 0.15 for the remainder. But this was all academic, the W&B having hardly any trade at this time and even if it had these rates would have killed it!

In 1894 Swindon New Town Local Board arranged to maintain the towing paths in its area; these could then be used as Public highways. In this year also the Syndicate manager and others carried out a detailed inspection of the T&S on behalf of the Allied Navigations of which the W&B was still a member. His own canal was practically disused by 1895 and an extra blow fell when the GWR started to obtain their water from Kemble; their yearly payment of £300 ceased abruptly.

In 1896 the business was again transferred, this time to a firm of boat owners at Bath and Bristol who failed and went into liquidation owing to losses. By 1898 there was no traffic on the eastern end and only 8,168 tons west of Swindon.

The first discussions about the inevitable closure had come in 1896 when several Swindon gentlemen held a private meeting suggesting that the Local Authority should take over the 3¾ mile portion of the canal within the Borough. No progress was made because of difficulties over approaching the Board of Trade. In the following year the Syndicate, at last convinced that the canal could not be made a commercial proposition, applied for a warrant of abandonment under the 1888 Railway and Canal Act. That April Swindon Traders Association approved the proposed closure as not only was the canal no positive use, but its many bridges interfered with traffic, services etc. The stagnant water was noisome, a danger to health and the cause of a number of deaths by drowning. They estimated the removal of the canal would free 1,500 ft of building frontage. Swindon New Town opposed closure claiming water rights, because the towpath had become a right of way and because they had built a wharf near Commercial Road bridge. Old Town followed suit.

Wiltshire County Council too opposed closure on the grounds of loss of water supply and the heavy compensation demands expected. Landowners also opposed as did the K&A and T&S both of whom had, in the past, gratefully accepted a lockful of water every time a boat passed Semington or Latton. Later in 1897 New Town UDC offered to buy the part of the canal in its area but although the Syndicate was practically bankrupt they would accept nothing less than £20,000, a sum not forthcoming.

In February 1900 the Board of Trade represented by Major General C.S. Hutchinson opened an enquiry at the Public Office Swindon into the abandonment application by which the Syndicate sought to obtain relief from "all liability to maintain the same canal, and from all statutory and other obligations in respect thereof." The 1888 Act required the Board to be satisfied that the canal had been disused for three years, or become unfit through the default of the Proprietors. The *Swindon Advertiser* pointed out that neither of these requirements was met and although the canal was "an abominable nuisance" in the town it was still useful for drainage and for watering cattle. This last point was also supported by the large number of landowners present at the enquiry. In reply to Objection 36 from the Stroudwater Navigation the Syndicate replied coldly,

> The T&S renovation is proceeding, and with the deepening and straightening of the upper Thames will provide better facilities than the W&B. There is no evidence that Traders in Swindon had any use for the NW. The Syndicate had offered the

NW to the T & S and then to the Sharpness Docks Committee but despite the alleged advantages neither would have it. The Committee of the T & S Trust know that as a connecting link with the Thames the W & B is entirely unnecessary.

The abandonment proposal failed finally on a technicality; the application applied to the whole canal but after the notice had been issued and during the arguments the T & S Trust entered into a provisional agreement with the Syndicate to keep open the NW from Latton to Rodbourne Road, Swindon, the maintenance of Coate and the supplying the branch with water therefrom and also the construction of a wharf at Rodbourne Rd. The proposal was therefore changed without a change of notice and on this point the enquiry was adjourned and never reconvened. Gloucester County Council who had taken over from the T & S Trust then repudiated the agreement but still required that the NW should be continued and maintained but in this hope they were to be disappointed.

In February 1901 Wiltshire County Council agreed that the importance of the W & B as a traffic route was not sufficient to justify them in acquiring it by purchase for the purpose of putting it in repair and opening it as a commercial waterway. They set up a committee to discuss water supplies with landowners and offered some sensible advice

> We desire to impress very strongly on all concerned that it is only by the recognition of fact, and through a spirit of compromise, that the canal can be rescued from its present objectionable condition, and the utmost advantage be taken of the existing water supply. An insistence on their extreme rights by each and all of the parties can only continue the existing deadlock, as the rights of each party can without difficulty be reduced to vanishing point by the combined opposition of the other parties. The ultimate result in that course could be only one of two things, either the canal will become entirely derelict and remain a nuisance to health in the towns and an obstruction in rural districts, or the Town Council of Swindon may succeed in passing a Bill of its own. It would be a strong argument for Parliament for such a Bill if it could be shown that through the opposition or indifference of other public bodies and private persons interested, an earlier scheme safeguarding the rights of all parties, and materially assisted by the Town Council itself, had had to be abandoned.

Despite this warning the deadlock continued. The Syndicate now wanted £16,500 for the whole canal, this the landowners refused to pay. They stated that they would not contribute one penny if the canal and Coate were either given up by the Syndicate or bought by someone else but they were prepared to contribute if another party would maintain the canal as a water channel only.

The 22nd November, 1901 edition of the *Wiltshire Mirror* reported, "the aqueduct over a branch of the River Avon, near Calne was washed away during the floods of last winter, the shareholders not being able, or perhaps unwilling to repair it and restore through communication."

J.A. Saner, when preparing his paper "On Waterways in Great Britain" presented to the Institution of Civil Engineers in 1905, wrote to all canal company Secretaries for reports on their concerns; Ainsworth's answer was "the traffic had decreased to the point at which any change must be for the better."

Swindon Corporation spent £1,500 in 1908 in dredging the 3¾ miles inside the Borough but it was soon choked again with weed, mud and rubbish. The stagnant water became foul and unhealthy in summer, not a pleasant background for two schools and the many houses nearby. The bridges on the main line, (from east to west, Drove Rd, York Rd, Whale, Golden Lion, Commercial Rd, Cambria, Marlborough Rd, Kingshill) and on the NW (John St, Fleet St, Bullens, Iffley Rd, Rodbourne Rd) were narrow and in a bad state of repair; few would allow the passage of boats if there were any. The Corporation could not blame the Syndicate for this as the bridges were built and maintained by themselves.

The Royal Commission on Canals and Inland Navigations of the United Kingdom presented its report in December 1909. It had little to add but repeats the sorry tale of the W & B,

> It was largely used within living memory for the transport of coal, corn, building materials and road making materials. Now it is absolutely unused and its banks are delapidated. The Company which owns it makes a small revenue, insufficient to meet expenses, by the sale of water. The stagnant condition of this canal makes it offensive to the people of Swindon and Abingdon and a desire has been expressed to close it altogether and fill in the bed. The closing is, however, opposed by the landowners for certain reasons, including the fact that their tenants obtain water from it for their cattle.

In 1912 yet another conference was held in Swindon attended by representatives of landowners, the County Councils of Wiltshire and Berkshire and Swindon Corporation. Although no comprehensive scheme emerged the Corporation felt justified in promoting a Bill in three parts (1) Preliminary (2) Concerning the canal in Swindon and Coate (3) Concerning the remainder, the NW and the Company itself. The latter agreed to support the Bill in April 1913 but only if both parts 2 and 3 were included; the Corporation thought that if 3 were not passed the case for 2 would remain. Wiltshire CC passed a resolution in August to take responsibility for bridges outside the Borough if the Bill were passed siding with the Company in requiring that both parts 2 and 3 be presented.

The Private Bill was introduced in the House of Commons in February 1914; it ran to 20 pages with 27 pages of amendments. A select committee was set up to examine the Bill and hear the views of the supporting and opposing parties. Lord Craven, the Thames Conservancy, Viscount Barrington and Charterhouse were prominent amongst the latter. For the Syndicate W.J. Ainsworth, the Manager, gave evidence and was cross examined. He answered a variety of questions concerning the canal stating that it originally had 165 bridges of various types, that the Newbury road bridge at Abingdon had been replaced by a solid embankment pierced by pipes to allow water to pass, that a portion of the Chippenham branch had been filled in, that the capacity of Coate reservoir was 125 million gallons and Tockenham 50-60 million and that the paid up capital of the Syndicate was £17,000. He recounted the history of the undertaking and described in detail the part Lord Wantage had played in financing the Syndicate. He stated that to prove that water from Coate was not necessary to supply water to landowners west of Swindon the Syndicate had built a temporary dam at the Borough boundry leaving Wroughton Brook alone to supply the flow west. The canal was dry in places, especially on the NW, bridges were dangerous, often blocking the canal, Rural and Urban District Councils maintaining many of them. Numerous locks were in a ruinous and unworkable condition and towing paths were overgrown. He submitted a series of photographs showing the present state of parts of the canal.

The Act received the Royal Assent on 31st July, 1914 as *4&5 Geo. 5 Cap. 108* "An Act to authorise the transfer to the Mayor, Aldermen and Burgesses of the Borough of Swindon the site of portion of the Wilts and Berks canal and Coate Reservoir and the abandonment of the remainder of such canal and the sale or disposal of the site thereof, and for other purposes."

Under part 2 Swindon Corporation acquired all the Syndicate property in Swindon, including Coate, for £10,000. This money was to be paid within three months and on payment the Syndicate was to be cleared of all liabilities in Swindon. Towing paths were to be rights of way and the Corporation could fill in the canal and make streets thereon. (The Corporation actually considered the site to be worthless apart from that occupied by the junction of the NW and the main line. Their estimate for filling in the canal was £40,000, of this £4,000 would be needed to pipe water from east to west to satisfy landowners and £5,000 to improve bridges.) They could sell or lease any canal lands, any money so obtained being used to offset their expenses. Coate reservoir became part of the Corporation water undertaking but its water could only be used on the streets. The area would continue to be used as a Public Park and charges and Byelaws made concerning its use.

The question of water supplies for landowners outside the Borough was controversial. Many claimed rights but the 1795 Act merely stated that should the canal be disused for 14 years its lands could be resold to the original owners or their successors, presumably in its original condition. It was first planned to send 50,000 gallons daily into the main line to the east, similiar amounts to the west and down the NW but by the time the Bill became the Act the flow to the east was increased to 200,000 daily. The NW which was practically dry anyway was to receive none and 50,000 to flow west entering the canal immediately beyond the dam at the Borough Boundary. These flows were to be measured. To the east the Thames Commissioners wanted water from Coate to follow its old course along the Rivers Cole and Ray to the Thames, water being pumped into the canal as necessary. This would have required more then the 200,000 gallons and ignored the fact that the Goddard lands along the feeder still had to be supplied. The Ecclesiastical Commissioners also wanted water to flow down Lotmead Brook for watering cattle and flooding water meadows in their estates; they were told they could have any excess water but the quantity could not be guaranteed. They could however obtain supplies from the Coate and Wanborough feeders, both under Corporation control.

The estates of Lord Lansdowne, Lord Crowe and Richard Carnaby Foster on the west side had the canal lands passing through their property vested in them and the water rights of Tockenham reservoir were to be disposed of by the Syndicate.

The dam west of the boundary was to be retained and maintained by the Corporation, the Thames Commissioners having access to it. The Corporation was also to build another dam at Summit lock to prevent any water flowing further west; this was to be maintained by the landowner. Water from Coate and as much as necessary from Wroughton Brook via the feeder from West Leaze could be used for agricultural purposes east of this dam, the Corporation having no control over the Brook.

East of the Borough the owners of land abutting on the canal had it vested in them free of charge together with rights to water. All bridges and land beside and beneath were vested in the Authority owning the roads on either side; should the bridge be replaced by an embankment provision was to be made for the passage of water. The GWR was vested with the sites of railway bridges and canal property beneath such outside the Borough and could improve bridges at its own expense, making provision for water flow.

The Syndicate was to be wound up when financial affairs were completed. From their funds they were first to pay £2,500 to road authorities for bridge transfers. The second payment was to F.P. Goddard a descendant of Ambrose. The two agreed rentals of £12 and £8 had lapsed, by 1914 he was owed £225. If this were paid within 2 years the Corporation could redeem the rent charges for 18 years purchase, £360. Lady Wantage received £7,000 in consideration of the £4,489 lent by Lord Wantage (who died in 1901) to the Syndicate in 1891 plus interest which had not been paid for over 20 years; the amount owing on this loan was almost £2,000 more than Lady Wantage received. The security mortgage on Coate could not be effected as it became Corporation property. No compensation was paid to her Ladyship in connection with her husband's £10,000 loan of 1891; no interest had been paid on this since 1895, possibly because in that year the income from water sales to the GWR had ceased. In all she was owed £16,000 – and received nothing. The last payment was to the Corporation for the expenses of the Act. Any other funds were to be used for winding up costs, further road authority compensation, other compensations including those for necessary mainte-nance work when land was not sold to the adjoining owner, and payments to shareholders. Any money remaining in Syndicate hands 6 months after the sale of lands was to be paid to the Paymaster General who would clear any remaining claims.

Thus died the Wilts and Berks canal which had started off with such high hopes but whose doom was sealed when the GWR decided to build their line alongside, and doubly so when supplies of Somerset coal diminished. How much their investments profited the original Proprietors by improved trans-port opening up their estates in the early days cannot be written down in cold figures, but there can be no doubt that while the W&B could not be called financially successful it did contribute materially to the prosperity and development of northern Wiltshire and Berkshire, providing the upper Avon valley and the Vale of the White Horse with a cheap supply of coal, mainly for domestic use though the textile mills of the Avon valley used a fair quantity in their steam mills.

As to the length of time for which it provided a useful purpose, this compares favourably with many of the railways built during the Railway Mania.

Finally, three factors contributing to the unsatisfactory finances should be noted. Financial crises following the Napoleonic wars increased the cost of the undertaking to three times that estimated. The calculated probable annual tonnage which would be carried was 233,644 tons. In fact, even in the most prosperous years, the amount was barely one third of this. The lack of balanced trade too was to be a great burden; over three quarters of the total trade was from west to east. Westward the boats returned empty producing meagre tolls but still using the same quantity of water and producing similiar amounts of wear and tear.

To the Proprietors of Shares in the Wilts and Berks Canal Navigation:—

Mr. Dunsford, the Gentleman, who for about Twenty Years has had the management of the affairs of the Wilts & Berks Canal Navigation Company, found the concern, when he took to it, not only profitless and unable to pay the Shareholders the smallest Dividend, but also nearly Twenty Thousand Pounds in debt:—by excellent management and the most assiduous devotedness of his great business talents to the rendering profitable the said undertaking, he not only succeeded in paying off the debt, but many years since, he commenced paying the Shareholders a Dividend which has annually increased in amount:—this year, (1839), there has been paid the Shareholders a Dividend of £1.10 p Share. As this great improvement is principally attributable to his exertions, many of the Shareholders are desirous of evincing their high opinion of Mr. Dunsford's merits, by promoting a Subscription for the purchase and presentation to him of a Piece of Plate suitably inscribed: and they take the liberty to solicit the concurrence of the rest of the Shareholders, in presenting their very efficient and faithful Agent with such an acknowledgement of his meritorious services.—

Subscriptions are respectfully requested to be made to the Treasurers, Messrs Strange, Strange & Co, Bankers, Swindon, Wilts. or on their account, to Messrs Masterman, Peters & Co, Bankers, London

A Golden Handshake!

Chapter Eleven
The W & B in 1985

Since the first edition of this book was published in 1971 the deterioration and infilling of the canal line has accelerated. All abandoned canal sites, particularly lock chambers and those near roads provide popular dumping grounds for rubbish of all sorts. The tendency towards larger fields has ensured that where the canal existed as a shallow trench with the spoil heaped low on either side the ubiquitous bulldozer makes reclamation a simple matter. Embankments and deeper cuttings present greater problems and are more likely to survive. As long ago as 1956 a British Waterways Board estimate for reclaiming a normal ground level course was £6,000 to £9,000 per mile.

Much of the remaining brickwork has deteriorated and such has been the growth of scrub and trees that many of the objects on view in 1970 are now completely obscured.

The whole line of the canal is covered by the 1:50000 Ordnance Survey maps 173 and 174 with the exception of the last few kilometres to Abingdon. However, not all the track shown can now be found.

The junction with the Kennet and Avon canal is just east of the A350 bridge over that canal at Semington (900 610). The masonry arch bridge carrying the K & A towpath over the entrance to the W & B has been filled in and cemented over. The original toll collector's house in in perfect condition and lived in, the regulating lock site being in its garden. Northwards there is no trace of the canal until some 150 metres on at 900 612, the site of a drawbridge once carrying a green lane across the canal to bypass a turnpike toll gate on the main road. Some brickwork remains. For 400 metres, up to the site of a bridge carrying the earlier Devizes branch of the Wilts, Somerset and Weymouth railway (901 615), the canal bed, overgrown but still watered, parallels the road.

The canal then swings to the east and then northward again running parallel to the road but 100 metres to the east. Most of the bed from here, through Melksham and beyond, has been filled but at Shail's Lane, 902 619, a short length survives as an ornamental pond in a garden. A low embankment crosses a brook at 902 624 but the culvert has been dug out. Elsewhere this has often been done to drain the derelict bed.

Through Melksham the canal line is usually marked by the remains of the towpath hedge and in many places a footpath still follows the course. Often the bed has either been built on or converted into gardens. An isolated embankment some 150 metres long (50 metres recognisable canal) carrying the course over Labburn's Brook can be found off Ruskin Avenue (908 641). At the junction of Forest and Calne Roads the parapet of a brick arched bridge survives.

North of Melksham, up to the embankment over Forest Brook at 914 656, all trace of the canal, including Melksham Forest lock and an arch bridge have disappeared. Beyond the brook with its brick and stone culvert 300 metres of bed are visible but beyond the lane crossing at 916 659 infilling is in progress. Either side of the track to Queensfield the canal is infilled but the bed can be found again at 924 666. From here to within 100 metres of the site of Laycock

Wharf at 926 680 (1.4 Km) the canal is substantially intact.

There is a delightful little culvert at 925 688; alongside a deep trench has been cut across the embankment. Queensfield lock at 926 670 is full of rubbish. The tail bridge is still in use. Just before the remains of Laycock Lock (927 674) the bed has been converted into a slurry pit. North of the lock are the remains of Stroud Bridge (927 676). Beyond the site of Laycock Wharf, now a garden, and over the road up to Ray Mill bridge at 926 689 (0.8 Km) the canal is either infilled or being converted into a pleasure garden by the owner of Bewley Court whose embankment is pierced by a brick culvert.

Beyond Ray Mill bridge site the bed is infilled for 0.5 Km reappearing at the remains of Nash Hill drawbridge at 926 694. Soon the canal is cut into the side of the hill overlooking the River Avon. The bed is dry and grassed over up to the brick arch of the unusually wide Double Bridge at 931 699.

The unfilled bed continues north east passing over two culverts, the second one over Cocklemore Brook earlier used, via a brickwork overflow channel, for regulating water levels. The one walled chamber of Pewsham Bottom lock is at 936 709. On the east bank is a wide shallow spillway and above a 100 metre semicircular pound with a stone wall on the west side leading to Pewsham Middle, somewhat decrepit, and finally Pewsham Top at 937 712.

Above the top lock a 0.5 Km length has been infilled. This included the junction with the Chippenham branch, now unrecognisable. At 941 715 the bed reappears and, apart from the A4 crossing at Forest Gate, 946 716, the infilled Studley Bridge at 958 722 and the embankment of the abandoned Calne branch railway nearby, is unfilled up to the junction with the Calne branch 2.4 Km away, just above Stanley Top lock (960 726). Just below Stanley Bottom lock at 960 724 are the sorry remains of the two-arched Stanley Aqueduct over the River Marden. The collapse of the south arch in 1901 was the final nail in the coffin of the W&B. Recently the other arch also showed signs of incipient collapse.

On the main line, 400 metres beyond the junction is the site of Stanley New Bridge at 959 729. Over the road 100 metres of the bed is filled but the bed then reappears and is unfilled to Bremhill Wick bridge site at 969 746. Beyond 350 metres has been filled as far as 972 748. A public footpath crosses at 974 749 the site of Bremhill Grove drawbridge. The bed is then clear up to the site of Foxham arch bridge at 982 773 passing the site of Charlcutt Hill bridge at 978 756 with its large unexplained basin by the road, the remains of two drawbridges, and a culvert at 983 764.

The two Foxham locks are a short distance north of the road, at 982 774 and 981 775, the track alongside being a public footpath. From the top lock the canal is intact for just over 1 Km to 980 786. Beyond and for another 1 Km all traces disappear. Included in this length is Wood Common lock buried in 1969 at 981 789. At 985 796, the site of City bridge, the canal reappears and is clear for 1.3 Km up to the A420 at Dauntsey lock. To the west of the road the wharf and canal houses built for Joseph Barnes, one of the principal users of the canal, lie derelict. Dauntsey lock, to the east of the road is buried and the canal infilled for another 350 metres to 998 802.

The next 4.2 Km of bed is intact up to 036 814, this section including Seven Locks (018 807 to 025 811). These are very overgrown and although the majority of bricks have been removed in the past, the sites of all chambers, intermediate pounds etc. can be found. The road at the former Bowd's bridge crossed the tail of the first lock up from the bottom. Above the top lock a former canal stable remains at the canal edge and the lock keeper's house survives. Trow Lane bridge at 024 811 provides a view of the 1 in 100 Wootton Bassett incline which lifts the railway up the same rise as Seven Locks lifted the canal.

The canal can be followed, with difficulty, to 036 814, the bed now carrying the overflow from Tockenham reservoir. From the road to 037 814, approximately 100 metres, is infilled. Another 350 metre filling extends from 042 817 to 045 818 passing Hart Farm bridge at 043 818, now in a precarious state. The next 0.8 Km holds water and is planted with bat willows, a commercial crop. At 052 816 Vastern Wharf site is covered by a wood yard. Improvements to the A420 (now A3102) have obliterated the canal beyond, the new line being in a cutting below canal level at 053 815.

There is little sign of the canal until 058 815 from where, on a rising embankment, the bed is intact up to 063 815, the site of Dunnington Bottom lock, passing over the deteriorating aqueduct crossing Thunder Brook at 062 815. 900 metres of infill cover Dunnington Top lock site at 066 815 from whence to 073 816 the bed is covered by gardens, the B4041 road crossing, and garages.

For the next 1.3 Km to 086 818 the bed is clear, from here to 088 818,200 metres of infill cover the site of Chaddington lock at 087 818. Beyond 0.7 Km to 095 815 the bed is clear and the site of Summit lock (092 816) readily discernable. The lock cottage alongside has been demolished as also has Chaddington Lane arch bridge at 095 815. Beyond, to 099 814, the canal line is now a drainage channel. Infilling starts again at 106 819, 500 metres short of Hay Lane Wharf site at 110 820. From here up to the aqueduct over Wroughton Brook at 137 833 Wiltshire County Council in 1962 filled the bed which ran alongside a minor road and crossed the later M4 at Wharf Farm (128 822). Wroughton Brook, headwater of the River Ray, was one of the original summit water supplies.

Beyond the aqueduct a beautiful skew brick bridge carried the now defunct Midland & South Western Junction Railway high overhead. From this bridge (137 834) the bed has been cleaned out and is watered up to 139 838, 200 metres short of Kingshill Rd., Swindon. It is strange irony that this section which gave so much trouble to the builders now holds water best of all!

Through Swindon the bed has been filled but not built on. Cambria and Commercial Rd bridges still span the track and on Fleming Way, following the canal line, the abutments of York Rd bridge remain. "Dunsford's Wharf" site now houses a fire station and in the Parade shopping centre a milestone "Semington 26 Miles" is a reminder of the former use of the site. From the roundabout at 160 849 a short infilled section with a stone footpath bridge survives.

Beyond the new A419 the canal is filled up to 209 873. Close by the road before Longleaze Farm the four Marston locks lie buried since 1960; a small part of the brickwork of the top lock remains. 560 metres beyond 209 873 a pile of debris is all that remains of the three 7 ft arched brick aqueduct once carrying the W & B over the River Cole at Acorn Bridge. Beyond, the southern arch of the GWR bridge, once the canal arch, now provides a second carriageway for the A420. The bed is then clear almost up to Cemetry Bridge site at 242 882 except for an infilled path crossing at 234 880. The B4000 bridge is intact, the only one on the whole length of the W & B.

At 244 883 the bed reappears and continues for 600 metres up to the infilled site of the former aqueduct over Beckett Brook at 249 886. The 7 ft arch has been destroyed but much brickwork remains. Apart from a 200 metre infill the bed is clear to Bowles bridge at 260 889. The culvert at 256 884 has been opened out. West of the bridge site some 50 metres is filled and occupied by a scrap dealer.

The canal is intact and clear past the junction with the Longcot branch at 267 893 to within 150 metres of Wharf Road crossing at 274 893. The west of the road Longcot top lock was buried in 1946. The earlier bridge here was a mechanically operated lift one. The Wharf House is a private residence.

To the east the canal appears in a cutting and can be followed past Longcot Bottom lock (280 895) to the former bridge under the GWR (282 894). Beyond the railway and up to 291 898 there are the remains of three bridges. Just as the canal appears to be about to dive under the railway again the bed has been ploughed over and all traces disappear. A footpath on Sheet 174 shows the path of the canal up to Uffington Bridge at 300 897 but this too is missing. Over the road the dry bed is on an embankment; the aqueduct over Woolstone Brook at 302 898 is punctured.

Further on, passing the sites of two lift bridges, Munday's and Thatcher's, the canal enters a deep cutting with large spoil heaps nearby. The canal approach to Uffington Arch bridge site (313 897) has been filled.

After this it is possible to follow the canal, past the site of Whitfield's and Stallard's bridges, to the site of Kingston Common Farm bridge at 330 889. Over the road the site of Keate's bridge is just before that of Broadleaze farm (341 889). At 347 888 the foundations of Sparsholt drawbridge are visible, the canal then entering a deep cutting before the site of the former B4001 bridge at 357 887. To the east the flooded bed has trees on either side. One field length has been partially filled, then, after the remains of Shippery bridge (363 882), the canal passes into a cutting where the site of Childrey bridge now carries a bridleway (365 882).

From West Challow bridge site (368 882) to East Challow ditto (380 883), passing the remains of King's lift bridge on Cornhill lane (375 883), the towpath has been cleared. A house straddles the bed before the A417 bridge site. Over the road the canal and cleared towpath can be found 200 metres on and followed to the site of Stockham's bridge at 390 888. Beyond, the bed soon enters a cutting filled with debris from the long disused airfield. Traces of the brickwork of Hunter's bridge can be found at 392 889. The approach to Barwell bridge has been levelled.

To the east of the site of Barwell bridge (394 891) the canal bed still performs its original function, carrying coal. A few yards on are the remains of Grove Top lock and the start of the infilled ¾ mile Wantage branch. Beyond there are well trodden paths on both sides of the bed, passing a wide section before reaching the remains of Limekiln lock. Wide sections like this are frequently found before locks, their function being to act as reservoirs for the 30 to 40 thousand gallons of water used in lockage.

Following the lock tail the canal embankment was levelled in 1969 but a footpath continues, passing the site of the former aqueduct over Letcombe Brook, up to the site of the earlier A338 bridge.

Across the road the canal can be traced past the back of the former Grove Wharf buildings, now named "Ormond Terrace", easily recognisable by the massive Swindon stone window and door surrounds. The nearby Grove Common lock can be reached by a signposted footpath crossing the A338. Both the lock and its tail bridge are in fair condition. Along the embankment to the east the canal has been filled and cultivated up to Smallmarch lock (409 898). The chamber is almost completely filled with tree trunks and household rubbish, a common fate for accessible – and sometimes inaccessible – locks!

Beyond the canal has been reduced to a clean drainage ditch at the end of which there are traces of the brickwork of Spirit lock. Eastward the bed carries on past the abutments of the vanished Crabtree Lane lift bridge soon reaching Grove Bottom lock at 420 901. The course beyond has been levelled but appears again at a farm crossing. To the right of the filled bridge a fancy culvert of stone carries a drain under the approach. The bed then continues to the road crossing at 423 903. The elegant iron bridge once here has gone but luckily a photograph exists.

Beyond, to the north east both sides of the still damp bed has been planted with willows, a commercial crop. A pleasant walk leads to a wide basin and then, almost surrounded by drainage ditches, Ardington Top lock. This is in very fair condition, the chamber, top culverts, paddle gear and bottom gates are all visible. Nearby are the sad remains of the lock cottage. At the tail of the lock there is a farm crossing. Soon the railway appears, the former bridge being replaced by an embankment. The canal curves to the north east, passing a milestone 46½ (miles from Semington) lying on the bank. Arding-ton March lock then appears; this is another fine example of a lock untouched since abandonment. The frame of the top gate, complete with its balance beam, is still in position but only one bottom gate survives.

The drain at 432 922 once dived under the canal, the culvert later being opened out to drain the bed. Not far beyond the canal has been filled in and the ground cultivated but a bridle path marks the line to the Cow Common road at 441 929. The former fine stone arch bridge at this point was demolished in 1965 to allow heavy loads to be carried to Didcot Power Station, then building. Across the road a concrete path leading to a large farm complex covers the canal line past the site of the buried Steventon lock (445 934). Beyond, up to the crossing at 447 936, the canal has been levelled. A bridle path alongside the unfilled bed beyond leads to Drayton lock (452 936) under a 10KV power line and with a farm crossing at the tail. The power line marks the continued but levelled line as far as 467 955 where the bed reappears and can be followed up to the busy Abingdon bypass, on the other side of which the filled bed can be followed up to the outskirts of Abingdon and beyond the foundations of a massive pill box to the remains of Tythe Barn lock at 485 965. From here to the A34 the towpath has been preserved as a series of interconnecting footpaths through a maze of new houses.

Beyond the A34 where the canal bridge had been infilled even before abandonment, the bed, long since filled in and grassed over, runs along Caldecot Road to the canal basin at the rear of the large brick building in Wilsham Road now (1985) occupied by Reynolds Office Equipment. No wharf buildings remain and the connecting lock with the Thames is buried under the entrance road. The curved stone walls marking the junction with the river form a convenient mooring recess for overwintering boats!

At St Helen's wharf nearby the cast iron bridge over the River Ock, specified in the 1795 Act but not installed until 1824, is still in use. It has been widened on the side away from the Thames to provide a footpath. Cast on the other side, in large letters covering the whole span, is the inscription; "Erected by the Wilts and Berks Canal Co. A.D. 1824. Cast at Acramans Bristol."

Of the principal W&B branch, the North Wilts, very little remains. The junction with the main line in Swindon has been completely built over. The course through the GWR works which included three locks has been converted into a broad footpath and cycle track passing under the extremely wide railway bridge. The fourth Swindon lock is buried under Rodbourne Road and the fifth just to the east. Most of the bed towards Moredon was filled with ash from Moredon Power Station, itself now gone without trace. On the site now cleared were Moredon Top and Middle locks and a lock cottage. The bed can be found at the road crossing at 122 873 and is clear up to the aqueduct over the River Ray at 114 878 passing the site of Moredon Bottom lock. The towing path is obviously in regular use. The east face of the aqueduct is perfect but the west side is deteriorating and portion of the northern of the three arches has fallen in providing an excellent vertical section of the four course brickwork.

Opposite the renovated Purton Wharf buildings, lovingly labelled "North Wilts Canal Cottage" can be found the remains of Pry lock and a short section of the bed and a wide basin (109 888).

One wall of Crosslanes lock can be seen in the front garden of the house at 106 897. Hayes Knoll lock and bridge are not to be found but to the south of the site some 100 metres of the bed are still clear and watered.

At 098 923 there is another aqueduct carrying the filled bed over the River Key. The canal crossed the road here and the bed beyond has been used as a rubbish tip and completely obliterated.

The cutting leading up to the south portal of the 100 metre Cricklade tunnel (096 931) has recently been filled and built over, no trace of the tunnel can now be seen. To the north the canal can be found alongside West Mill Lane at the end of which the towpath is impenetrable. A footpath carries straight on, crosses two branches of the Thames and then continues along the north bank of the river. The canal on the other side has been filled, reappearing before the site of an aqueduct over the river, now replaced by a wooden footbridge. Much brickwork remains on either side of the gap and the foundations of the three original arches are easily visible in the river bed. Further on the towpath crosses another footbridge where another aqueduct has been demolished. All the W&B aqueducts, with the exception of that over the Marden, were massive constructions of stone or brick carrying the canal on its bed of earth and puddled clay over very low and small arches allowing the river or stream to pass underneath. The design was James Brindley's and was basically a culverted embankment.

Latton lock cottage has been renovated and extended. The regulating lock was built on the aqueduct stipulated by the Act to pass flood water; the chamber is partially filled but all details are visible. Latton Basin is dry; it is 70 metres long, 20 metres wide and 2 metres deep with walls of massive stone blocks. The abutments of the former stone aqueduct over the River Churn are visible, so is the entrance to this from the Thames and Severn canal, unfilled at this point. The site can be approached from the A419 down the private lane from 090 956.

The kilometre long Wantage branch has been infilled and built on. The Wharf site at the bottom of Mill St still contains all the original buildings. The Wharfinger's house is built of large stone blocks. Another building, a mixture of stone and brick bears a plaque "1830". The arch of Belmont bridge built under the 1795 Act has recently been demolished to make room for new housing.

The Longcot branch, 1.2 km long, is unfilled; the wharf basin, 90 metres by 8, with a winding point at its entrance, remains and the wharf building is now a private dwelling.

Little remains of the 2.5 km level Chippenham branch. The deep cutting approach to the town and the 90 metre tunnel were filled in 1970. One canal building remains on the site of the wharf, now a bus station.

The Calne branch is 5.1 km long. 200 metres from Stanley Junction the centre of the arch of Carpenters bridge has collapsed and a low level concrete slab bridge gives farm access. For some distance the canal remains perched on the hillside and one fields length before Hazeland Mill bridge (972 723) has been filled. Beyond the watered bed can be followed through Hazeland Wood. The aqueduct of a tributary of the Marden at 977 718 has been demolished. Beyond one wall of each of the Conigre locks at 982 713 and 980 714 remain. The following 1 km past the site of the former tunnel under the A4, buried during road realignment in 1967, has been filled up to 988 708.

The final 1.1 km from here to Calne lock is the subject of a restoration project by the W&B Canal Amenity Group and the Calne Civic Society. There is a causeway for farm vehicles at 990 709 and then Chaveywell bridge (995 708), a brick arched structure. Calne lock is intact for most of its length but is obstructed near the top end by a large storm drain. Above, the canal joined the River Marden; this was a major water intake point, supplying the Calne and Chippenham branches and the main line from Foxham southwards. 200 metres of the river were navigable up to the site of Calne wharf, now a car park, all the original buildings being demolished in 1970.

South of Swindon Coate reservoir is still a public park much frequented by the citizens' of Swindon. There is a rather superior diving board erection in the lake but the "Bathing in the lake is forbidden" notice severly inhibits its usefulness. Pollution is the reason though fishing and boating are not affected. The walled off feeder arch is inscribed "1822".

The area around Chaveywell Bridge is now well used for water-based events and for recreation by the Calne townspeople. *D.G. & B.A. Small*

This fixed bridge was built by the local landowner, but will eventually be rebuilt as a lift bridge to allow for navigation. *D.G. & B.A. Small*

The Wilts & Berks Canal Company own about two miles of canal and have restored the derelict cottages at Dauntsey. *D.G. & B.A. Small*

Dauntsey lock, seen here in 1997, has now been completely rebuilt. *D.G. & B.A. Small*

The canal, drained in early 1998, exposing the sewer pipe which obstructed navigation. Wessex Water removed the pipe before the start of the 1998 Trailboat Rally.   *D.G. & B.A. Small*

The 1998 Trailboat Rally brought 50 boats onto the water at Templar's Firs. The boats had a mile of clear canal to cruise.   *D.G. & B.A. Small*

Beavan's Bridge, June 2000, at West Leaze near Swindon. This will be the first new stone-arch bridge built over the canal in living memory. *D.G. & B.A. Small*

Skew Bridge, June 2000, at West Leaze near Swindon. The canal has been dredged and the tow path reinstated. A cycleway passes over the bridge. *D.G. & B.A. Small*

On Moredon aqueduct the brick arches had to be almost completely rebuilt. This entailed the damming of the River Ray and working in very wet conditions underneath. *D.G. & B.A. Small*

Work in hand on the Elm Farm section near Wantage in 1995. This is between Grove Top lock and Lime Kiln lock. *D.G. & B.A. Small*

Chapter Twelve

Into the 21st Century
by D.G. Small

In 1987, a dramatic change of policy by the Wilts & Berks Canal Amenity Group (W&BCAG) had a profound effect on the fortunes of the canal. From just trying to preserve what remained of the old canal, the group decided that full restoration, using as much of the old line and infrastructure as possible, was practical. They had no doubt of the magnitude of the task before them, but were confident that a restored Wilts & Berks Canal was essential to the Wessex Waterway Network, forming, as it does, the central section. In the succeeding years, nearly 10 per cent of the canal, at several different sites, has been restored and a number of structures have been either restored or rebuilt.

It is impossible in one chapter to itemise everything that has occurred so far on a restoration of this scale. A separate book would be needed. Choosing a few of the successful projects and achievements will, I am sure, show that confidence in the success of the project is fully justified.

From 1988 onwards, work commenced at several sites led by members of W&BCAG and aided at times by other organisations. One of these was the Waterway Recovery Group (WRG) who for many years had been assisting canal restoration projects all over the country. In 1991, WRG was 21 years old and they were looking for a suitable site for a 21st anniversary 'Big Dig'. They chose a two mile stretch of the W&B canal near Wantage. Over 1,000 navvies turned out for the weekend and impressively cleared the canal line, much to the surprise of many local people who had not known it was there. The 'Big Dig' generated a great deal of positive publicity and goodwill. Since the 'Big Dig', Grove Top lock has had the wing walls rebuilt and the surrounding area landscaped. The pound between it and Limekiln lock, known as Elm Farm, was officially opened in 1995. An attractive length at East Challow has been dredged and is in water and work has begun at West Challow. Some clearance work has been carried out at Childrey and Grove Common lock tail bridge has been rebuilt.

A commercial company was formed in the early 1990s, called the Wilts & Berks Canal Company (W&BCC), to purchase approximately two miles of canal either side of Dauntsey lock and the derelict cottages alongside the canal. Although not connected to W&BCAG, the Company has given its full support to the restoration and has, with assistance from volunteers, restored most of its canal to water, rebuilt Dauntsey lock, built a new spillweir and restored a second. The Company's major commercial concern was the successful restoration of the cottages which are now inhabited.

Early in 1997, a trust was formed known as the Wilts & Berks Canal Trust (W&BCT). The members of the Trust were North Wilts District Council, West Wilts District Council, Swindon Borough Council, Vale of the White Horse District Council, Oxfordshire County Council, Wiltshire County Council and W&BCAG. This was an important milestone as it formally involved all the local authorities along the canal line. Late in 1998, a feasibility study (commissioned by W&BCT) was published and confirmed that there were no insurmountable problems preventing full restoration. Following on from this, a strategic study was undertaken and the results of this study are now being implemented.

In October of 1997, BBC Television's *Close Up West* was making a documentary about the Kennet & Avon Canal and, requiring extra footage of adjacent waterways, spent a day filming at various locations. This ended up as a 10 minute section in the finished production including interviews with various W&BCAG Directors and the Chairman of W&BCT. Two of the sites where the BBC filmed were significant. On the restored section at Templar's Firs, near Wootton Bassett, a water pipe obstructed through navigation and urgently needed to be removed. At Moredon, on the North Wilts branch, work was nearing completion on the aqueduct over the River Ray. This aqueduct is probably the largest feature on the canal and had to be almost totally rebuilt. The Inland Waterways Association (IWA) had selected the Templar's Firs section to be the site of the 1998 National Trailboat Rally which explains the significance of the water pipe. Wessex Water, the responsible authority, removed the obstruction and re-laid it beneath the canal bed. This was done in a spirit of co-operation and on very reasonable financial terms. The boat rally was officially opened by David Bellamy and the three-day event was an enormous success.

The recently formed Cricklade Country Way Trust (CCWT) is an added boost for the canal and especially the North Wilts section. The CCWT's aim is to form a leisure corridor including the Swindon and Cricklade Railway (the old MSWJR), part of the North Wilts Canal, footpaths, a cycleway and a bridleway. Ambitious plans include combined historic train and boat trips through the corridor.

In Melksham, there has been a continuing discussion about the most appropriate route to take to enable the canal to join the Kennet & Avon. This may now have been finally resolved. Clearance work in the Forest Farm area is now proceeding at a encouraging rate. Early work at Foxham resulted in the complete rebuilding of Foxham Top lock and the construction of a fully operational traditional lift bridge. More bridge building, clearance and dredging is currently under way. At Calne, Chaveywell Bridge has been rebuilt and several hundred metres of canal restored. This is one of the places that proves the popularity of restored waterways. Water-based events here, such as the summer Canal Day and the winter Santa Cruise, always attract large crowds. As this is the only remaining arm on the canal, Calne will be an important destination for future boaters and an ideal location for a marina. Dunnington aqueduct has been partially restored and plans are well advanced for the rebuilding of Summit lock. At West Leaze the canal has been dredged both sides of the Skew Bridge (the MSWJR bridge) and Beavan's stone bridge is being rebuilt. This will allow the newly watered section to be connected to the length of canal previously restored by a local farmer and currently a very popular fishery. As well as the fully restored aqueduct on the North Wilts, Mouldon lock has been rebuilt and the canal dredged back to Purton Road. In the very near future, a navigable culvert will be built under this road, linking two sections of canal for the first time since abandonment. Needless to say, alternative canal routes will be required to the west and south of Swindon. These have been identified and provisionally agreed. During 1998, a canalside park was completed alongside the canal in Shrivenham. Hundreds of trees were planted and, with the aid of WRG, a slipway built into the canal. Further dredging and the rebuilding of Steppingstones Bridge are the current projects in this area. Around Abingdon, progress is slow while we wait for a final decision from Thames Water as whether or not they intend to build a new reservoir. If built, this will straddle the line of the old canal which will then be re-routed during the construction of the reservoir. The final route for the canal to reach the River Thames is still subject to discussion.

The Wilts & Berks Canal is coming back to life and will certainly become an integral part of the Wessex Waterways Network. When that will be depends on many factors, such as the will of local government, the availability of funds, the successful completion of negotiations with landowners and, most importantly, the continuing dedication and enthusiasm of W&BCAG members. The work of the Group takes many forms from the actual work on high profile projects such as Moredon, Dauntsey and Shrivenham to organising special events like the Trailboat Festival. Members of the Council of Management, branch officials and officers with specific responsibilities spend much of their time organising the day-to-day business of the group. We must also not forget the various worksites along the route where, every week, the volunteers are making steady progress improving the amenity value of the canal. Always in the background, people are using their skills, knowledge and contacts to promote the restoration to commerce, Government and the public.

Now that the Kennet & Avon is fully open, it has become obvious that the Wilts & Berks is one of the new millennium's foremost restoration projects; it certainly is the longest at over 60 miles. There are great opportunities already for ramblers, photographers, birdwatchers and so forth, to explore the line of the canal. However, for whatever reason, it must be remembered that much of it is still private property. The leisure and economic possibilities presented by the prospect of the fully restored W&B, North Wilts and Thames & Severn canals linking the waters of the River Severn, the Kennett & Avon and the River Thames are immensely exciting and would have been of great satisfaction to Jack.

Jack Dalby passed away in 1990. His contribution to our knowledge of the canal and the resurrection of this almost forgotten and nearly lost waterway cannot be overstated.

Thank you Jack!

The Wilts and Berks Canal Amenity Group

The aim of the group is to protect, conserve and improve the route of the Wilts & Berks and North Wilts Canals, and branches, for the benefit of the community and the environment, with the ultimate goal of restoring a continuous navigable waterway linking the Kennet & Avon Canal at, or near, Melksham, the River Thames at, or near, Abingdon, and the Thames & Severn Canal at, or near, Cricklade.

The immediate objectives of the Group are:

To convince local authorities, government departments and local organisations of the benefits and feasibility of the proposed restoration.

To convince landowners, local commerce and the general public of the merits of the restoration.

To secure the route of the waterway and adequate water supplies.

To establish the Amenity Group as a key member of the partnership with local authorities and other bodies that will facilitate restoration of the canal.

To implement an agreed programme for full restoration of the canal.

The group was formed at a meeting in Swindon in October 1977. Jack Dalby was the first President of W&BCAG. There are now nine active branches whose members work on, and take responsibility for, different sections of the canal. The group's membership has continued to grow over the years reflecting the increased interest in canal restoration in general and restoring the Wilts & Berks Canal as part of the Wessex Waterway Network in particular. New members are always welcome. Further information about the group can be obtained from:

Chris Toms, Membership Secretary, 16, Firham Park Avenue,
Harold Wood, Romford, Essex, RM3 0SJ
Information line   01 628 544666
Web site http://web.ukonline.co.uk/dg.small/index.htm

EPILOGUE

The old canal, from bank to bank,
Is filled with reeds and rushes rank;
And down this lane of living green
March memories of what has been.

The painted barges came from town,
And busy life flowed up and down.
But there is nothing left to show
Where those old barges used to go.

Progress is always marching on;
The old canal is dead and gone,
But still we seem to hear it say,
"I, too, was Progress – yesterday."

Reginald Arkell

Appendix One

The Enabling Act

The Enabling Act, *35 Geo. 111 Cap. 52*, received the Royal Assent on 30th April, 1795 and was entitled

> An Act for making and maintaining a Navigable Canal from the River Thames or Isis, at or near the town of Abingdon, in the County of Berks, to join or communicate with the Kennet and Avon Canal, at or near the Town of Trowbridge, in the County of Wilts: and also certain navigable Cuts therein described.

These cuts are specified in the preamble as branches from Grove to Wantage, from Bremhill to Calne, and from Pewsham to Chippenham; that later built to Longcot is not mentioned.

There is a certain similiarity between all the Canal Acts of this period, for the reader who is not familiar with these it may well be worth while noting the powers granted by the Act, remembering that many of these are common to other Acts.

The preamble sets out in the usual glowing terms the virtues of the work,

> Such a Canal and branches will greatly facilitate, and render more convenient and less expensive than at present, the Conveyance of all Kinds of Commodities, not only to and from several Towns near the Lines of such Canal and Cuts, but also to and from the Ports of London and Bristol, and will be of great Public Utility.

The Proprietors are to be united into a Company by the name of "The Company of Proprietors of the Wilts and Berks Canal Navigation." The list of 138 such Proprietors includes the Marquis of Landsdowne and the Earls of Clarendon, Peterborough, Radnor and Carnarvon.

> Water may be taken from all such springs as may be encountered in excavating the canal, and also from all rivers, springs, brooks, streams and watercourses which are or shall be found within the distance of 2,000 yards from any part of the canal or branches, or from any reservoir to be made as described later. If necessary weirs, steam engines and other machines with proper shafts and tunnels thereto may be erected to supply water. [There are a number of exceptions to these powers.] No water (except for puddling) should be taken from the Avon or its tributaries between Trowbridge and Stanley Abbey or from certain other specified streams, in all cases these should be crossed by aqueducts or culverts. No water is to be taken from Tockenham Water, Trow Lane Water or Wootton Bassett Brook between 10th June and 10th September yearly except from the last named should it be overflowing its banks. Where taking water diminished the value of Meadow lands the Company must pay compensation, and if any Mill is deprived of its source of power the Owner may compel the Company to purchase it. The water for the Summit level is to be obtained from the supplies of Wanborough Mill by means of a feeder, and from a reservoir in Coate Valley which may be fed by any waters flowing into the valley. In building this reservoir only certain parts of the lands belonging to William Dyke and John Stone shall be taken, and a dam built to protect the remainder of these lands. Further, water can be taken from the brook running through the south east branch of the valley, but when such water is not required it should be allowed to run in its old course and be conveyed under the reservoir through a proper and sufficient drain, culvert or tunnel.
>
> The Company must provide watering places for cattle to replace existing facilities, and must not infringe existing water rights. They are to puddle the sides of the canal to prevent seepage, make drains to convey water from adjoining lands and keep these clean, if they neglect to do so Landowners may clean them at the Company's expense, similiarly the Company may clean adjoining ditches at the Owner's expense should they neglect to do so. In the case of damage caused by floods, and for preventing further damage the Company may immediately enter lands near the canal to repair such damage.
>
> The Company is authorised to enter any lands to survey and take levels and there to bore, dig, cut, trench and carry away earth &c., to set up bridges, tunnels, soughs, aqueducts, sluices, locks, flood gates, weirs, reservoirs, drains, wharf quays, Toll houses, warehouses, watch houses, landing places, weighing beams, cranes, dry docks, fire engines or other machines, ways, roads, towing paths, turning and passing places, their workmen doing as little damage as possible and repairing same, the Company making financial satisfaction to Owners etc. No trees should be cut down unless in the direct line of the canal, and no houses, gardens etc are to be taken without the Owner's consent.

Maps or plans describing the line of the canal and the names of the Owners of lands to be crossed should be deposited with the Clerks of the Peace in Wiltshire and Berkshire for public inspection. The course of the line is laid down in certain lands. The width of towing path and canal should not exceed thirty yards excepting where docks, basons or reservoirs shall be made, or where embankments or cuttings are more than six feet high or deep, or at passing or turning places or where warehouses, cranes or wharves are built, at these places the total width may be 100 yards. Exceptions are on waste ground or common land or where any Landowner may require it to be wider, the expense of this to be borne by the Landowner.

Commissioners are to be appointed to settle any disputes about the purchase or conveyance of lands, compensation for damages etc. If any piece of ground cut off by the canal is less than one acre in extent or less than 50 yds wide it shall be purchased by the Company if the Owner so requires.

All works must be adequately fenced, the Commissioners to decide where gates and bridges must be provided, public rights of way must be preserved, and where any road is to be cut a suitable crossing must be provided. Bridges must be built in Abingdon at Caldecot Farm, over the exit to the Thames and over the river Ock close by. The Company must erect and for ever afterwards maintain and keep in good repair a commodious and substantial carriage bridge of brick or stone over the Wantage branch in view of Belmont House belonging to Samuel Worthington Esq., and another proper and carriage bridge close to Grove Top lock in the lands of the same gentleman. The rate of ascent or descent to any statutory bridge is not to be greater than three inches perpendicular to every yard horizontal. Should the Company not build these specified bridges or neglect proper fencing, the Landowners may do the same at the Company's expense. They may also erect bridges etc. at their own expense, subject to the permission of the Company.

All top soil removed to the depth of nine inches to be replaced over any under soil spread over lands adjoining the canal. If the Company refuse to do so then the Landowner may do so at the Company's expense, this does not apply to lands on yearly lets or where the Landowner does not require such preservation of the top soil.

The Company reserve the right to build inclined planes instead of locks if it should be deemed expedient to do so.

The Company has powers to raise £111,900 amongst themselves, this capital to be divided into 1,119 shares, initially no person may hold more than 50 or less than one share. This sum is to be used to pay the expenses of this Act, the cost of making surveys and preparing plans, and finally in paying for the making and maintaining of the canal and associated works. All shares are to be numbered and the names of the Proprietors owning them entered in a register, as a receipt he shall be given a certificate bearing the same number as his share and with the Common Seal of the Company affixed. Shares are to be regarded as Personal Estate and holders are entitled to receive a proportion of the profits according to the number of shares held.

Should this capital prove insufficient the Company may raise a further £150,000 either amongst themselves or by Mortgage. Shareholders will be paid interest at the rate of 5% per annum from capital until the work is complete provided that the interest on Mortgages is first paid.

For the purpose of electing a Committee of Management the Proprietors will be divided into two sections, each electing five members. The first section includes those resident in Berkshire, London or any county north of the Thames and the line as far as Wiltshire and Gloucester, they will be called the Proprietors of the Berkshire District and hold annual general meetings at the Bear Inn Wantage at which their five members will be elected. The remainder of the Proprietors will be called the Proprietors of the Wiltshire District holding their meetings at the Town Hall Wootton Bassett. The ten members so elected will meet at the Crown Inn Swindon to choose another five members from the Proprietors at large.

At these meetings to elect a member of the Committee of Management or to elect a Treasurer no person shall have more than 50 votes in person or by proxy even though he might by means of any mill or settlement hold more than 50 shares. In all other voting nobody will have more than 10 votes in person or 5 by proxy. At all meetings the appointed Chairman shall have the casting vote. Any member may be re-elected, but no person holding any office or place of profit can be a member of the Committee, a member may be disqualified also by being absent from three successive Committee meetings without sufficient excuse.

The Committee of Management will meet every three months at Swindon, notices of these meetings will be issued to the newspapers of Wiltshire and Berkshire. They will elect a

Chairman and call a General Meeting to elect a Treasurer who must lodge sufficient security before he be permitted to receive any money. The Committee will elect a Chief Clerk, Engineer, Toll Collectors etc. taking security from those handling money, the accounts of these officers will be audited at a General Meeting in June.

The Committee may make calls for money as necessary, no such calls shall be more than £10 or more frequent than every two months, 28 day's notice of such calls being given in the newspapers of Wiltshire and Berkshire and in certain London papers. They have power to purchase land, agree compensation, enter into contracts etc. and are to keep accounts of receipts and disbursements, and minutes of all proceedings, their expenses will be defrayed by the Company, they have full powers to make byelaws, rules and orders considered necessary for the good government of the Company.

Proprietors failing to answer a call will be fined £5 for each share, and after three months in default shares will be forfeited after due notice has been given.

If any Proprietor owning more than 300 shares is dissatisfied with the Treasurer he may call a General Meeting to discuss the cause.

The Company is empowered to take the following rates and Tolls for tonnage:–

For all Hay, Straw, Dung, Peat, and Peat Ashes, and for all other Ashes, intended to be used for Manure, and for all Chalk, Marle Clay and Sand, and for all Lime intended to be used for Manure, and for all other articles intended to be used for Manure, and for all Materials for the Repair of Roads, any sum not exceeding One Halfpenny per Ton per Mile;

For all Coals, Culm, Coke, Cinders, Charcoal, Iron Stone, Pig Iron, Iron Ore, Copper Ore, Lead Ore, Lime (except what shall be intended to be used for Manure) Lime Stone and other stone, Bricks and Tiles, any sum not exceeding One Penny Halfpenny per Ton per Mile;

For all Corn and other Grain, Flour Malt, Meal, Timber, Bar Iron and Lead, any sum not exceeding Twopence per Ton per Mile;

And for all other Goods, Wares, Merchandise and Commodities whatsoever, not before specified, any sum not exceeding Twopence Halfpenny per Ton per Mile;

All tonnage is to be paid in Proportion for any greater or less Quantity than a Ton, or greater or less Distance than a Mile.

The Company shall erect posts or marks at each half mile, Tolls are to be paid for the full half mile even if a boat shall not actually complete the half mile, and where loads do not make up an even quarter ton they are to be charged for the next full quarter. Boats carrying Hay, Straw or Corn in the straw, road repair material or any kind of manure passing any lock when water is not flowing over the waste weir shall pay an extra Toll of one halfpenny per ton mile. Persons evading payment of the higher Tolls when not exempted therefrom shall, if convicted, forfeit and pay to the Company £5 for every such offence. To simplify the tonnage payable on timber and light goods it is specified that 40 cubic feet of round or 50 cubic feet of square oak, ash, elm or beech, 50 cubic feet of fir, deal, poplar or birch and 60 cubic feet of light goods shall be deemed to be one ton weight. Goods remaining on wharves for more than 48 hours will be charged extra.

Rates and Tolls are to be paid to Persons appointed by the Committee, goods may be seized and boats detained until Tolls are paid, and if not redeemed within five days they may be sold. Taxes on the Tolls are to be apportioned amongst the Parishes in proportion to the length of the canal in them, but no tax is to be paid until the Company distributes a dividend of 5%.

Masters of boats must furnish an account in writing of the goods on board to the Toll Collectors, those neglecting to do so or unloading goods at any point not specified will be fined £2. In the event of a dispute the Collector may detain a boat and cause it to be weighed, measured and gauged, and if the weight is greater than stated the Owner shall pay for the gauging,and similarly if equal to or less the Company shall pay together with such damages as may have arisen.

The Company may from time to time vary the Tolls, but not raise them above those laid down in this Act, they must keep a true account of costs of all sorts for making the Canal, for its maintenance, and of all Tolls etc. and issue a Balance Sheet on May 29th yearly.

The Canal will not be subject to the Commissioners of Sewers.

All boats shall have the Owners name, address and number painted thereon, Owners must register their numbers with the Clerk. A certificate of gauging will always be carried. Staging between bank and boat must be used when unloading, the penalty for infringement of any of these rules will be £2. Owners of boats are answerable for damage done by their boats, horses or servants.

All locks must be left empty, upper and lower gates and sluices must be opened in the correct sequence and not both together. If another boat is in sight the lock need not be emptied or the bottom gates closed. Boats going up shall have priority over those coming down. A number of boats waiting to rise and descend must do so in turn so that each lockful of water should serve two boats. Lock keepers are not to give preference to boats passing locks or using wharves. No boat of less than 20 tons is to pass locks without written consent unless the tonnage for 20 tons is paid, but two boats capable of entering a lock together and of carrying 20 tons are to be treated as a single boat. Boats causing obstruction may be removed by the Company and fined ten shillings plus five shillings for each hour the obstruction continues. Boats sunk may be salvaged by the Company and held until all expenses are paid.

Any person loading or unloading other than at Private or Public Wharves with intent to avoid paying Tolls or without first having obtained permission will be fined £1 to £5.

If any swivel or drawbridge be opened to allow the passage of a boat it must be closed after such passage, the penalty for leaving one open or opening one when no boat is to pass will be £5.

Further penalties may be levied for floating timber on the canal without permission, for using boats with loads obstructing navigation, for throwing rubbish into the canal, for drawing off water or leaving lock gates or sluices open.

Persons destroying canal banks or other works will be liable to transportation or such punishment as the law directs in cases of petty larceny.

Lords of Manors and others may erect wharves etc. on their own lands for their own or Public use, Tolls may be collected for the use of the same on the same scale as by the Company. If the Company requests in writing that such wharves, roads etc. be built for Public use and the Owner does not comply within one year, then the Company is empowered to build them paying for land taken. The Company may not use any Private wharf without permission, Owners of such wharves may not demand more than 3d per ton for any merchandise landed, or 1d per ton on goods left thereon for more than six days.

Fishing rights are reserved for Owners of land through which the canal passes, but the Company shall not be responsible for fish killed by repairs or works. Owners and occupiers of lands may use pleasure boats or boats for the purpose of husbandry, or carrying cattle or manure from one part of a farm to another without paying any Tolls, such boats must not be over 5 ft wide and 12 ft long and not use any locks or obstruct navigation in any way.

If the Company shall be in possession of any lands purchased by them under this Act for 14 years without using the same, or if the canal is built thereon and afterwards discontinued or disused for the space of 14 years, then the Company shall immediately after the expiry of the 14 years reconvey the lands back to the original Owners or their successors, if they so wish, at the original price, if the Company refuses or neglects to do so then the land shall automatically revert to the original Owners, and if rents have been paid the rental should cease and any damages paid for.

If powers to raise more money are needed then an Act may be sought to do so as directed by a two thirds majority at a special meeting of Proprietors.

The Kennet and Avon Act of 1794 authorised branches from that canal to Calne and Chippenham and as it was proposed by several persons to build a canal from the Kennet and Avon to Abingdon also with branches to these towns, it was enacted that the execution of the powers of the Kennet and Avon respecting these branches be suspended for 2½ years. If within this time the subscribers of the canal from Trowbridge to Abingdon obtained their Act, and such branches were made within seven years then the Kennet and Avon's powers to make these branches should be void. It was enacted in the earlier Act that this Act should therefore contain a clause obliging the subscribers to complete the branches to the said towns of Calne and Chippenham, or within the distance of 100 yards of the same within seven years, they must also complete the line from such branches to the Kennet and Avon within the same time. If the branches are not completed in this time then no Tolls may be collected on any part of the Wilts and Berks.

The Kennet and Avon, finding since their Act that it would be less expensive if they adopted a shorter and more direct line from Foxhanger to that part of Lady Down Farm near Trowbridge where the Wilts and Berks is intended to join their canal, and carry the same to a close of meadow ground near Semington through which the said Wilts and Berks will pass and from thence along the same line to Lady Down Farm which is herein directed to be purchased in making the said Wilts and Berks; the said Kennet and Avon will apply to Parliament to adopt the new line and if so allowed the Wilts and Berks are willing to give up to them the portion of their line between Semington and Lady Down, the Kennet and Avon paying all expenses which shall have been incurred in taking and making several levels and surveys and purchasing land.

It is obvious that the conveying of coals from the Somerset coalfield down the Thames to Reading and beyond would be detrimental to the coasting trade so it is here enacted that no coal passing along the Wilts and Berks should pass beyond Reading on pain of forfeiture of any boat and its cargo of coal so passing.

This Act is to be deemed and taken as a Public Act.

Appendix Two

Rules, Orders and Byelaws

RULES, ORDERS and BYELAWS made by the Committee of Management of the Wilts & Berks Canal Navigation at their General Quarterly Meeting held on the Sixteenth day of June 1819 for the well and orderly using of the said Navigation and for the orderly behaviour of all Bargemen, Boatmen and Others employed or to be employed thereon.

1. That no boatman or other person shall navigate any boat upon this Canal at any other times than between the hours of seven in the morning and five in the evening during the month of November, December, January and February, between the hours of five in the evening and seven in the evening during the months of March, April, September and October, and between the hours of four in the morning and nine in the evening during the months of May, June, July and August, nor on any Sunday, Christmas Day or Good Friday without the consent of the Company's superintendent for the time being.

2. That no boat shall pass any lock or be navigated upon any part of this Canal which shall have a square head or stern or any projection at the sides or bottom thereof or be constructed in any respect so as to injure the locks, bridges, masonry, banks, lining, puddling or other works of the said Canal except by the special permission of the Committee of Management of this navigation or their Superintendent for the time being but the same will be prevented from passing any lock or navigating the said Canal by any of the Lock-keepers or servants of the said Company.

3. That no boat shall be navigated upon any part of this Canal with the stern foremost (except in passing to the nearest turning place) or without a rudder and that the rudder shall be made upon such construction and hung in such manner as in no wise to injure or tend to injure any of the works of the said Canal and the Steerer or person having the care of any boat navigated contrary to this Byelaw shall for every offence against the same forfeit and pay any sum not exceeding forty shillings nor less than twenty shillings.

4. That no person or persons shall navigate on this Canal two or more boats fastened together whether loaded or unloaded but that each boat shall be haled by one horse only with the haling line fixed to the mast and the person employed to drive the horse shall be of the age of fourteen years at the least and there shall be another person of the age of eighteen years at the least at the rudder to steer or guide such boat and the steerer or person in care of any boat navigated contrary to this Byelaw shall for every offence against the same forfeit and pay any sum not exceeding Forty Shillings nor less than Twenty shillings.

5. That no boat or other vessel having on board any pole, shaft or other instrument used or intended to be used in punting or navigating such boat or other vessel, pointed, spiked or shod with iron or other metal of less area at each end thereof than ten square inches shall pass upon any part of this Canal and the steerer or person having the care of any boat or other vessel on board of which such poles, shaft or other instrument shall be found for every such offence forfeit and pay any sum not exceeding Five Pounds nor less than Twenty Shillings.

6. That every empty boat passing on this Canal shall give way to every loaded boat until the loaded boat shall have cleared such empty boat and all loaded boats travelling towards Abingdon shall have passage given them by those boats going in a contrary direction and the steerer or person in care of any boat navigated contrary to this Byelaw shall for every offence against the same forfeit and pay any sum not exceeding Forty Shillings nor less than Twenty shillings.

7. That every person having the command or care of every boat shall before the same arrives at any swivel or drawbridge over this Canal cause such bridge to be effectively opened and shall so steer his boat as to prevent it from striking and injuring the platform, handrail or any other part thereof and any person offending against this Byelaw shall forfeit and pay any sum not exceeding Five Pounds nor less than Forty shillings.

8.   That the steerer or person in care of any boat navigating on this Canal shall on approaching any lock thereon cause the horse to be loosened from the line by which such boat shall be haled before the time such horse arrives at the beginnings of the wing walls thereof and shall pass his boat through any such lock without the use of the horse and that a strap or rope of sufficient strength shall always be attached to the stern of every boat and which the steerer or other boatman or person having the care thereof shall throw round a post for that purpose properly affixed in such manner as to check the too rapid progress of the said boat and prevent it from striking against the gates or other works of such lock and any steerer or person as aforesaid offending against these regulations and pay any sum not exceeding Five Pounds nor less than Twenty Shillings.

9.   That no boatman, lock-keeper or other person shall draw up or let down any paddle of a lock on this Canal without using a windlass for that purpose on pain of forfeiting for every such offence any sum not exceeding Forty shillings nor less than Twenty shillings.

10.   That no boatman or other person shall take into or discharge from any boat or other vessel the whole or any part of the lading thereof from or upon the bank of any aqueduct or whilst such boat remains in the chamber of any lock or within the distance of fifty yards of any aqueduct, lock or bridge on this Canal except from any regular wharf which may be within the said distance or except with the consent in writing of the Company Superintendent for the time being.

11.   That every boatman or other person having the care of any boat or vessel not navigating the same on the Canal, moor and fasten or cause to be fastened such boat at both ends on the opposite side of the Canal to the towing path, but that no boatman or other person shall tie up any boat within fifty yards of any lock, bridge, aqueduct or stop gate.

12.   That no person or persons wilfully unmoor or unfasten any boat or cause the same to be adrift.

13.   That no person or persons may make a road across, pull up, make gaps in or in any way whatsoever injure or destroy or cause to be injured or destroyed any part of the fences of the towing path or other works of this Canal.

14.   That no boatman or person in care of any boat navigating on this Canal shall suffer the horse or other beast employed in haling the same to pass along the towing path thereof without being sufficiently muzzled at all times to prevent such horse or other beast from eating or cropping the quick or other fences belonging to the said Canal or shall suffer such horse or other beast to trample upon or in any way injure the same upon pain of forfeiting for every such offence any sum not exceeding the sum of Twenty shillings.

15.   That no horse infected with the glanders, mange or other contagious disease shall be employed to hale boats or for any other purpose on the line of this Canal and the steerer or person having the care of any boat which shall be haled by any such horse or the person using such horse in any other way on the said Canal shall for every such offence forfeit and pay any sum not exceeding Five Pounds nor less than Three Pounds.

16.   That if any person should wilfully throw in any carrion or other nuisance or shall bathe in any part of this Canal or shall angle or fish with nets or otherwise without being entitled to do so by the Act for making the said Canal, every such person shall forfeit and pay any sum not exceeding Five Pounds nor less than Twenty shillings.

17.   That no person navigating a boat upon this Canal shall pass any lock or stop gate thereon without delivering his Permit to the Toll Collector for that purpose appointed in order that the same may be examined and compared with the lading of such boats.

18.   That if any person shall wilfully and maliciously break open or cause to be broken open any padlock or other fastening of any lock or stop gate, bar or chain belonging to this Canal; or if any shall draw the paddles of or attempt to pass his boat through any lock during the time such lock is under repair or during the time that part of the Canal in which such lock is situated is shut up either for the purpose of repairs or of regulating the water belonging thereto, every such person offending against this Byelaw shall forfeit and pay any sum not exceeding the sum of Five Pounds.

19.   That no person shall use the towing path of this Canal except for the purpose of haling the boats navigating thereon nor shall any person or persons load or unload any boat from upon or carry or convey such loading across the towing path without the express leave of the Company's Superintendent first obtained in writing.

20.   That if any horse or other grazing beast shall be found loose on the towing path of this Canal except in such cases where the lands adjoining the same are not fenced off from the said towing path or except with the permission of the Company's Superintendent, the Owner or other person in care of such horse or other grazing beast shall forfeit and pay any sum not exceeding the sum of Twenty Shillings nor less than Ten Shillings.

21.   That if any person shall needlessly and wantonly open or draw up any swivel or drawbridge on this Canal or shall wilfully leave any gate open upon or adjoining the towing path thereof, every such person offending against this Byelaw shall forfeit and pay any sum not exceeding twenty shillings nor less than ten shillings.

22.   That at all wharves and other places upon this Canal where coals, goods, merchandise, materials and other things are landed out of or into boats there shall be a wall built or piles driven and a stank, stage or landing erected that boats may be fastened close to the side to be loaded or unloaded there, and that all coal, goods, merchandise, materials and other things which shall be unloaded at any wharf or other place in the side of the said Canal shall be placed at least five feet back from the edges of the stank, stage or landing to be erected.

23.   That any boat coming up to a wharf, as soon as it is brought to its station shall be haled to the side and fastened at both ends and be discharged of its lading with all convenient speed and that no boat after having completed its loading shall remain at such Wharf or upon any other part of the Canal longer than one hour without proceeding to the place of its destination provided that the time for its departure be reasonable and according to the regulations of the first Byelaw.

24.   That the steerer or person having the care of any boat or other vessel coming into any bason or adjoining any Wharf or Warehouse belonging to this Company shall tie up and moor such boat or other vessel in such place and manner as the Company's Wharfinger for the time being shall direct, and that all coals, goods, wares, merchandise or other things unloaded or to be unloaded at any Wharf or deposited in any Warehouse belonging to this Company shall be laid and placed in such manner and on such part of the said Wharf or in the said Warehouse as the Company's Wharfinger for the time being shall direct.

25.   That every carriage coming to any Wharf belonging to this Company for the purpose of being unloaded or unloaded shall after a reasonable time for such loading or unloading be removed as the Company's Wharfinger for the time being shall direct and that such carriages as are intended to be weighed at any of the Company's machines shall be weighed thereat in rotation according to the order in which they have entered the said Wharf, and not cross each other to gain a preference in turn.

26.   That the hours of doing business at the Wharves and Warehouses belonging to this Company shall be the same as those for navigating boats upon the Canal and that no boatman or other person shall remain upon such Wharves or in such Warehouses after the expiration of the said hours upon being required to quit the same by the Company's Wharfinger for the time being, and that no lighted candle shall at any time be used in the Company's Warehouses except in a lantern and then only with the permission and in the presence of the Company's Wharfinger for the time being.

27.   That no boatman or other person shall be allowed to sleep in the night in the cabin or on board of any boat within any of the Company's Wharves upon the Canal and that no fire be allowed to be made in any boat lying in the said Wharves without the permission of the Company's Wharfinger for the time being.

28.   That any person or persons having the care of or belonging to any boat navigating on this Canal shall in the presence of any Toll Collector, Lock keeper or other Agent or Servant of the Company infringe any of the foregoing Rules, Orders and Byelaws, it shall be lawful for such Toll Collector, Lock keeper or other Agent or Servant to lock the paddles of the next or of any lock or to fasten any stop gate, bar or chain, so as to prevent such boat passing until the case has been investigated before a Magistrate or until such person or persons shall make reparation for the enquiry ordained by the Company.

29.   That no Toll Collector, Lock keeper or other Servant of this Company shall under any pretence or colour whatsoever ask, demand, or receive for doing or executing any part of the business incident to his office or employment by the Company, any other pay or gratuity whatsoever than what shall be paid him by the said Company of Proprietors.

30.   That every person guilty of any breach of any of the foregoing Rules, Orders and Byelaws where no particular penalty is specified in the same shall for every such offence forfeit and pay to the Company any sum not exceeding Forty Shillings.

31.   That all persons convicted in any penalty under either of the aforesaid Rules, Orders and Byelaws shall over and above the same pay all the expenses attending such conviction provided the said penalty, fees and expenses shall not altogether exceed the sum of Five Pounds.

In Testimony whereof the Said Committee of Management have hereunto affixed the Common Seal of the Company of Proprietors of the said Canal Navigation, the day and year first above written.

General Directive.

For the Toll Collectors, Lock keepers and workmen employed by the said Company throughout the line of the said Canal.

They are respectively required to take notice that the several Rules, Orders and Byelaws as above written are observed and obeyed by all parties whomsoever within their several departments as far as they are able, and they are respectively required to give earliest information of any offences committed by any person or persons within their knowledge or observation in order that the offender may be punished according to law and in all cases of doubt or difficulties they are required to consult the Company's Principal Clerk or Superintendent previous to proceeding, and these instructions they are required strictly to observe on pain of the Company's displeasure.

Jas. Crowdy, Principal Clerk.

(COPY HELD BY WRO)

Appendix Three
Tolls

Before	1803	£889		1816	£6,290	1830	£9,755	1844	£8,545
	1803	£651		7	£8,476	1	£10,599	5	£8,874
	4	£2,029		8	£7,222	2	£11,131	6	£8,570
	5			9	£8,508	3	£10,897	7	£8,525
	6	£2,160	½ year	1820	£2,044	4	£10,972	8	£7,864
	7	£2,021	¼ year	1	£3,054	5	£11,489	9	£6,875
	8	£3,350		2	£7,724	6	£12,552	1871	£2,883
	9	£3,104		3	£9,900	7	£12,887	1876	£1,158
	1810	£3,164		4		8	£12,798	1882	£800
	1	£2,507		5		9	£15,531	1888	£843
	2	£5,765		6	£10,965	1840	£24,001	1891	£617
	3	£5,518		7	£10,232	1	£19,389	2	£569
	4	£6,386		8	£10,719	2	£9,565	3	£603
	5	£5,964		9	£10,287	3	£8,591	1904	£2.8s.6d

Appendix Four
Dividends

1812	£2,550	
1831	£4,000	
2	£5,000	
3	£5,000	
4	£5,500	
5	£5,500	
6	£6,250	£305.10s.0d spent on buying own shares.
7	£7,000	£648 spent on buying own shares.
8	£7,500	
9	£8,000	£1519 Tockenham Reservoir.
1840	£9,000	£429 shares, £3384 Tockenham Reservoir, £3,500 Reserve.
1	£9,000	£570 shares, Bourton wharf built.
2	£6,000	
3	£5,000	
4	£5,000	Thames wharf Oxford bought, £2077 from Reserve.
5	£5,500	
6	£5,500	
7	£4,913	
8	£3,438	
1853	£2,456	
1863	£1,128	
1870	£561	Final

Appendix Five

Tons of Coal Carried

TONS OF COAL CARRIED FROM SEMINGTON TO:

	Melksham	Laycock	Chippenham Stanley	Calne Foxham	Dauntsey	Wootton Bassett	Wroughton
1838	2840	657	4393	3916	1745	3141	808
1840	2800	1245	7232	4648	5052	8693	756
2	3280	991	4544	5095	2819	2878	647
4	3681	761	4165	4350	1909	2511	828
6	3965	655	6828	4207	2206	3169	1183
8	3336	843	7254	4725	1570	2798	1092
1850	3701	760	8752	4719	1994	2361	1148
2	4048	755	8237	4872	1964	2372	1193
4	4979	848	9587	5467	2564	2293	1426
6	3003	1037	8681	6174	2579	1134	1311
8	3318	1388	8933	6412	2551	1326	1450
1860	3373	1408	8899	7341	2962	1206	1029
2	3075	1276	7648	7612	3461	1216	757
4	2619	1286	6588	5725	3212	816	1062
6	2542	1289	6629	5853	2872	915	656
8	2347	1264	5463	5587	3001	1240	830
1870	1483	1338	3907	5019	2624	979	636
2	1511	1358	2785	4305	1683	794	519
4	786	663	2263	3136	890	793	466
6	723	649	3075	2133	1162	637	461
8	688	633	1745	1147	585	716	867

Records cease 15th Feb. 1879.

TONS OF COAL CARRIED FROM SEMINGTON TO:

	North Wilts	Swindon	Stratton	Marston	Bourton	Shrivenham	Longcot
1838	1952	2814	624	220	462	546	2804
1840	1587	3420	2809	774	685	601	2436
2	2166	3652	1308	—	312	330	1602
4	1991	2116	1308	574	632	271	1206
6	1799	4251	1255	136	682	490	2111
8	1450	2970	1878	—	823	272	2930
1850	1407	2888	1806	—	310	272	1995
2	1909	1522	1975	28	168	28	2257
4	2462	2464	1704	—	164	—	1768
6	2436	1775	1987	—	54	—	1157
8	2010	2035	1474	—	—	27	1026
1860	2624	1601	1652	—	—	—	1044
2	2156	1628	1218	—	75	—	1062
4	1376	1022	863	—	109	24	592
6	1691	1410	993	—	180	—	409
8	1621	892	1019	—	151	—	145
1870	1472	761	664	—	—	—	109
2	1608	905	421	—	—	—	58
4	713	415	354	—	—	—	3
6	839	466	123	—	27	—	—
8	239	678	278	28	—	—	26

TONS OF COAL CARRIED FROM SEMINGTON TO:

	Uffington	Challow	Wantage	Abingdon	TOTAL
1838	546	1668	1885	9930	40,961
1840	546	2279	1937	8369	55,869
2	520	1423	1902	8002	41,491
4	520	1215	2352	6736	37,525
6	504	972	2516	7201	44,736
8	686	912	2857	7143	43,262
1850	706	244	2806	6470	42,339
2	648	426	2690	5991	41,085
4	722	475	2761	5358	44,875
6	492	584	2618	3581	38,603
8	344	415	2160	2285	37,127
1860	320	652	2829	3641	40,861
2	280	773	3031	2623	37,892
4	123	307	1873	1478	29,075
6	80	179	2049	1297	28,994
8	170	291	2152	1044	27,137
1870	102	93	1068	340	20,595
2	80	122	1386	501	18,037
4	12	—	1402	152	12,048
6	—	22	1938	196	12,461
8	26	30	1904	152	9,775

Appendix Six
Number of Boats

NUMBER OF BOATS PASSING EITHER END OF SUMMIT, AND ENTERING AND LEAVING
THE NORTH WILTS BRANCH

	CHADDINGTON		NORTH WILTS		MARSTON	
	East	West	East	West	East	West
1841	1482	1420	361	320	1270	1207
2	1227	1220	403	383	978	945
3	1057	1110	269	276	996	923
4	1144	1064	217	228	1002	882
5	1148	1128	310	306	1010	966
6	1106	1094	190	183	785	778
7	1173	1135	198	191	864	818
8	1026	992	189	195	747	736
9	952	905	197	191	692	662
1850	893	872	202	212	645	590
1	829	819	137	142	567	604
2	862	837	246	246	589	615
3	1019	1009	151	166	642	628
4	885	864	186	201	535	497
5	818	834	231	256	584	515
6	745	709	188	199	502	466
7	932	926	191	206	493	438
8	704	699	185	204	455	386
9	798	846	186	203	521	459
1860	832	834	239	259	524	469
1	777	779	179	207	436	427
2	807	808	215	236	533	546
3	794	783	164	168	479	485
4	640	649	126	128	306	310

Appendix Seven
Tons of Moira Coal

TONS OF MOIRA COAL ENTERING AT ABINGDON:

1843	740	1850	204	1860	315
4	924	1	334	1	326
5	854	2	27	2	262
6	745	3	196	3	418
7	737	4	224	4	384
8	539	5	281		
9	368	6	284		
		7	347		
		8	353		
		9	352		

Appendix Eight
Coal passing from North Wilts

COAL PASSING FROM NORTH WILTS TO, (TONS):

	West of Swindon	Swindon	Longcot Uffington	Challow Wantage	Abingdon
1837	26	—	120	285	534
8	37	53	104	284	584
9	—	30	48	88	258
1840	1619	4386	36	2085	7471
1	685	199	—	273	314
2	325	457	30	151	548
3	28	182	—	20	248
4	47	181	—	12	144
5	104	688	20	157	366
6	2	302	—	98	288
7	93	540	—	365	173
8	545	902	158	344	96
9	310	626	210	356	138
1850	250	609	159	179	166
1	228	500	81	248	46
2	717	1073	309	224	305
3	26	368	278	283	396
4	—	20	92	95	73
5	26	51	—	97	72
6	—	25	53	110	88
7	—	—	30	121	127
8	24	—	—	50	124
9	—	23	—	84	87
1860	21	55	—	157	61
1	—	54	—	—	—
2	57	—	—	—	34

The increase in 1852 was due to a decrease in toll to 1/- per ton, this was raised to 1/8 in 1853 with a resulting decline in trade.

Appendix Nine
Coal Tonnage

NUMBER OF TONS ON WHICH DRAWBACKS WERE PAID:

	SOMERSET COAL			FOREST COAL	
	Above *Iffley*	*Below* *Benson*	*Below* *Pangbourne*	*Below* *Benson*	*Below* *Pangbourne*
1826	833	1966	1429	521	179
7	318	1048	561	171	109
8	230	860	135	566	65
9	166	139	179	—	—
1830	264	1615	52	154	—

Appendix Ten
Locks

	DISTANCE FROM ABINGDON		LOCK RISES		DISTANCE FROM ABINGDON		LOCK FALLS
	Miles	*Fur-longs*			*Miles*	*Fur-longs*	
Abingdon			9ft 6in.	Summit	30	2	8ft 0in.
Tythe Barn	0	6	9ft 2in.	Chaddington	30	5	7ft 10in.
Drayton	2	4	9ft 11in.	Dunnington Top	31	6	8ft 9in.
Steventon	4	0	9ft 4in.	Dunnington Bottom			8ft 3in.
Ardington March	5	3	9ft 5in.	Seven Locks 1	34	1	8ft 6in.
Ardington Top	5	6	9ft 5in.	Seven Locks 2			8ft 1in.
Grove Bottom	7	1	9ft 9in.	Seven Locks 3			8ft 10in.
Spirit			8ft 5in.	Seven Locks 4			8ft 10in.
Smallmarch			9ft 5in.	Seven Locks 5			8ft 6in.
Grove Common			9ft 3in.	Seven Locks 6			8ft 8in.
Limekiln			8ft 9in.	Seven Locks 7	34	5	8ft 9in.
Grove Top			8ft 5in.	Dauntsey	36	3	8ft 8in.
Longcot Bottom	14	6	9ft 5in.	Wood Common	37	7	9ft 0in.
Longcot Upper	16	4	9ft 0in.	Foxham Upper	39	1	9ft 1in.
Marston Bottom	21	2	7ft 8in.	Foxham Lower			9ft 2in.
Marston No 2			8ft 6in.	Stanley Top	42	7	7ft 11in.
Marston No 3			7ft 7in.	Stanley Bottom			9ft 2in.
Marston Top	21	7	7ft 3in.	Pewsham Top	45	1	8ft 9in.
				Pewsham Middle			10ft 1in.
				Pewsham Bottom			10ft 1in.
				Laycock	47	5	9ft 6in.
				Queensfield			8ft 0in.
				Melksham Forest	49	1	9ft 7in.
				Semington	52	1	1ft 8in.

North Wilts branch lock rises.

Latton	Regulating.
Hayes Knoll	6 ft 1 in.
Crosslanes	5 ft 5 in.
Pry	5 ft 0 in.
Moredon 1	5 ft 0 in.
Moredon 2	5 ft 8 in.
Moredon 3	5 ft 3 in.
Swindon 1	5 ft 3 in.
Swindon 2	5 ft 7 in.
Swindon 3	6 ft 0 in.
Swindon 4	5 ft 3 in.
Swindon 5	4 ft 7 in.

Calne branch

Calne wharf	
Conigre Top	Not known, total fall 21 ft.
Conigre Bottom	

Chippenham and Wantage branch both level.

Appendix Eleven

Hidden away in Book 39 in Swindon Reference Library are some interesting statistics of the trade for the years 1893–6 compiled by the United Commercial Syndicates Manager W.J. Ainsworth.

TABLE 1. SUMMARY OF TONNAGE BETWEEN WHARVES, 1893–6

Swindon – Abingdon	454	Challow – Abingdon	49
Abingdon – Swindon	469	Latton – Wantage	275
Uffington – Abingdon	27	Wroughton – Wantage	11
Swindon – Wantage	303	Uffington – Swindon	77
Childry – Abingdon	5	Sparsholt – Grove	45
Grove – Abingdon	814	Bowd's Br. – Swindon	26
Longcot – Abingdon	55	Semington – Sparsholt	99
Semington – Wantage	1327	Semington – Abingdon	5
Stratton – Wantage	30	Semington – Longcot	21
Bourton – Swindon	26	Marston – Wantage	55
Semington – Challow	51	Hay Lane – Wantage	9
Abingdon – Wantage	1477	Shrivenham – Wantage	48
Melksham – Bourton	123	Longcot – Swindon	227
Bourton – Wantage	59	Grove – Swindon	11
Abingdon – Chippenham	704	Ashbury Br. – Wantage	37

TABLE 2. TRADE AT WHARVES AND CARRIERS

		1893/4	1894/5	1895/6
Melksham	Independent	734	299	40
	Company	750	308	394
	Hiskins	294	1483	2480
Lacock	Ind.	46	472	260
	Co.	76	107	35
	Ainsworth	—	—	217
Chippenham	Brinkworth	696	605	525
	Co.	732	63	73
	Ind.		76	

	Ainsworth	—	—	37
Calne	Harris	190	544	590
	Co.	36	16	34
	Ainsworth	81	—	—
	Ind.	—	383	27
Derryhill	Ind.	238	321	344
	Co.	5	20	64
	Ainsworth	—	—	167
Tytherton	Ind.	69	109	—
	Co.	4	2	½
Stanley	Ind.	120	168	224
	Co.	24	3	—
Charlcutt Br.	Ind.	—	59	129
	Co.	2	4	—
Foxham	Ind.	520	371	681
	Co.	24	11	17
Dauntsey	Ind.	314	315	325
	Co.	12	3	8
Waites Hill	Ind.	—	77	88
Bowds Br.	Ind.	—	37	115
Seven Locks	Twine	—	72	—
	Ind.	—	6	—
Trow Lane	Hiskins	230	220	71
	Co.	5	15	13
Tockenham	Ind.	193	187	85
	Co.	175	239	104
Vastern	Twine	—	522	408
Chaddington	Twine	—	25	38
Wootton Bassett	Twine	750	158	10
	Co.	57	57	42
Hay Lane	Twine	197	310	—
	Ainsworth	—	—	87
	Co.	43	10	75
Wroughton	Ind.	16	—	4
	Co.	8	5	30
Swindon	Kurray	2022	2491	3171
	Ind.	173	170	169
	Co.	948	535	675
	Ainsworth	—	1205	833
Stratton	Ind.	20	14	1
	Co.	138	168	431
Latton	Ind.	376	213	87
Cricklade	Ind.	—	274	74
Hayes Knoll	Ind.	—	105	70
Moredon	Ind.	—	60	—
Marston	Ind.	28	20	—
Shrivenham	Ainsworth	—	23	—
Bourton	Ind.	22	101	—
Sparsholt	Ind.	—	37	63
Challow	Ind.	30	—	52
	Co.	10	—	—
	Ainsworth	—	46	19
Wantage	Ind.	1141	492	1140
	Co.	176	97	84
	Ainsworth	—	246	40
Grove	Ind.	249	350	255
Abingdon	Ind.	411	153	79
	Co.	5	—	—

TABLE 3. TOLLS ON EASTERN END

1893/4   £218.4s.10d
1894/5   £100.6s.5d